Lessons for a Lifetime

Children's Stories We Never Outgrow

Maureen Kasdorf

"A children's story which is only enjoyed by children
is a bad children's story."
–C.S. Lewis

Lessons for a Lifetime: Children's Stories We Never Outgrow
Copyrighted © 2020 Maureen Kasdorf
ISBN 978-1-64538-140-2
First Edition

Lessons for a Lifetime: Children's Stories We Never Outgrow
by Maureen Kasdorf

For information, please contact:

Orange Hat Publishing
www.orangehatpublishing.com
Waukesha, WI

Cover Design: Morghan Lamansky
Writing Coach: Kerri Lukasavitz, author of *Mystery Horse at Oak Lane Stable*

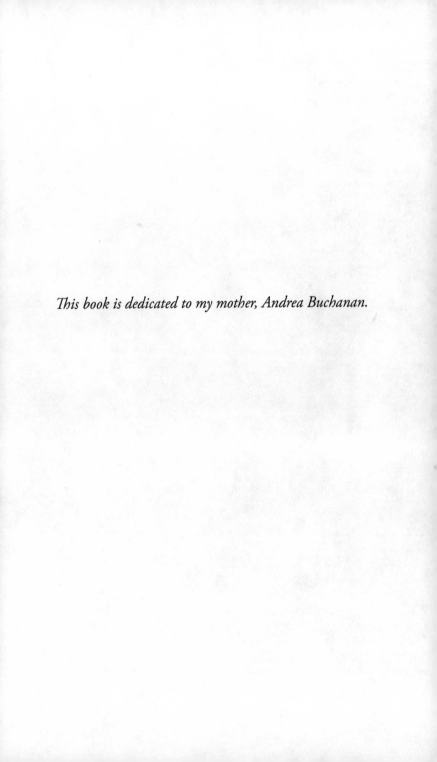

This book is dedicated to my mother, Andrea Buchanan.

TABLE OF CONTENTS

INTRODUCTION

As I dropped my older son off at soccer camp today, he looked at me uncertainly. None of the friends he thought would be there had showed up. He was surrounded by lots of children, but he still felt alone. This feeling isn't unique to our kids and, in fact, can grow more intense as we age. But what if we could bring someone we knew well with us to all those unfamiliar places and situations? What kind of friend could help us get through new encounters with confidence and reassure us that we are not alone? Someone who loves us best of all, perhaps? Occasionally we have a friend for a season and then, for whatever reason, we lose touch. If we are very lucky, that friendship might be rekindled along the way. Do you recall Corduroy the bear or Mike Mulligan and his steam shovel, Mary Anne? Could they possibly still be good company? Maybe even friends for other stages in life? Friends for life?

I believe that a good book, a good story, can cure nearly all ills. For me, stories have been a healing means of escape or an antidote to my problems through a new perspective. As solutions, some of the books I love show me a path of processing my problems so that I can move forward. The books I have included in this collection have offered me gentle encouragement and have been just the right medicine as I revisited them in adulthood. Most of these stories are part of my family's shared vocabulary, perfect to relate to our situations and feelings. Some days are "Alexander" days from *Alexander and the Terrible, Horrible, No Good, Very Bad Day.* Some nights Mom, like Mrs. Peters from *The Seven Silly Eaters,* "drearily shakes her head and wearily goes up to bed." I offer these beloved stories to you so that they might become part of your shared language too.

I included some of these stories because their voices are under-represented yet necessary and important in the greater conversations of my life and at this time in history. In this quest, I sought to elevate women authors and authors of diverse ethnic backgrounds in hopes that their stories become part of our collective classics.

While fiction has always been a remedy for me, I struggle to finish non-fiction. I read it, I do, because grown-ups must. But I get stuck. My nightstand is anchored by a stack of non-fiction books that others have recommended or that I have said I "need" to read. But the struggle is real! With this in mind, I hope that you will feel free to pick this book up, read a particular chapter and, should you decide to stop there, put it down. My goal is that you would revisit these timeless tales and beloved characters expecting a fresh reading, looking for the lasting nugget of advice. Perhaps this time when you revisit Max in his wolf suit from *Where the Wild Things Are* you would be able to see and understand that Max is actually processing anger in a prescriptive way. To help this process, each chapter includes current research, conversations, and expertise. Incredibly, I managed to finish a number of non-fiction books in my research for each chapter! I want to show you that our dear character friends can still show us relevant truths. Also, at the end of each chapter, I have included the titles of several other books with similar themes. Maybe, like me, you will discover new favorite stories after reading this book.

The realm of children's literature is vast, and I have many favorite chapter books. For this project, I narrowed my focus to only picture books. What I love about picture books is that a large problem is distilled within a small commitment of time, solutions are discovered, and the protagonist is changed by the conclusion. And there are pictures! Sometimes the message is best understood in fewer words.

My hope is that you would re-enter into the world of children's stories with these chapters, gaining fresh vision for your life and new resolve, cheered on by these old and new character friends.

CHAPTER 1

Catharsis

Alexander and the Terrible, Horrible,
No Good, Very Bad Day
by Judith Viorst

———

"When you read a book as a child, it becomes part of your identity in a way that no other reading in your life does."

–Meg Ryan's character in *You've Got Mail*

If you haven't heard of this book, or haven't picked it up in many years, then today is the day. You can even plan your evening around it! Feel free to check it out of your local library, but I am warning you, you will probably want to own a copy. After all, you can't *plan* to have "one of those days," so you should have a copy on hand, just in case. If not for you, then for someone you love.

In Judith Viorst's 1972 classic, a school-aged boy, Alexander, has a rough day. The pictures and comforting repetition of this story will carry you back to that often-pervasive feeling that life isn't fair, your siblings are out to get you, you never get what you want, and mom is so, so mean. Maybe you still hate lima beans or choo-choo train pajamas. Maybe you still remember how much it hurt to be someone's third-best friend. Maybe you've even tried going to Australia, and some days are still like that. This chapter is for you!

Every page of this book contains a list of the tiny insults and injuries that Alexander accumulates as he goes about a normal school day. And in typical childishness, his focus is only on his own suffering. Simultaneously, his mother isn't immune to Alex's plight. As a mother myself, I would argue that it is sometimes hard to have a wonderful day if your child is (loudly!) having a rough one. As the mother of a very dramatic child, I struggle not to laugh at the molehills which become mountains in the eyes of my daughter,

Liesel. In these moments, I'm sure my face looks much like Alexander's mother's expressions of annoyance, incredulity, exasperation, anger, and desperation.

As a parent, I often think of Alexander's mother on that "very bad day." Her day could very well have gone something like a recent day of mine—I overslept because my alarm was still on daylight savings time, I can't find anything to wear that fits or makes me look just the right combination of professional, chic and hip, the kids are whining, the dog peed on the carpet, we're out of coffee creamer, and my son's favorite pants are in the dirty clothes hamper. Of course, it's also trash day, and I forgot to take the cans to the street. When we finally leave, the car is running on fumes and the kids are still fussing. I'm ready to go back to bed! What does your very bad day look like?

Since grown-ups have bad days, too, I find it helpful and encouraging to read through Alexander's story again. When we have a terrible, horrible day, sometimes we just need to wallow in self-pity for the day, post the details on social media, and share our misery with anyone who will listen. When we have an Alexander kind of day, we have two choices—we can laugh about it or cry about it. At our house, we most often try to laugh. Who knows, Alexander's dramatically bad day was probably fodder for good-natured ribbing within a few years. In childhood, my husband, Mike, had one of those days. He announced to the family, whenever asked to do something, "I can't. I feel like crap." Years later, his family still quotes those words and everyone has a good laugh.

When we have an Alexander kind of day, we need a healthy way to process it. I believe we need to have this wonderfully relatable story in our arsenal so we can see the over-exaggerated terrible day, join our sorrows with the narrator, exorcize our excessive emotions, and see the ridiculousness of our initial feelings. We can recall all the feelings of being rejected, chosen last, or overlooked and acknowledge how it felt. This is called catharsis. It is a purging of emotions, purification, and sometimes a renewal resulting from pity, sorrow, sympathy, or even laughter. Catharsis can apply to the experience of a character or the experience of the audience. I would argue that in *Alexander*, our healing comes through our own catharsis.

Aristotle said catharsis is "a purgation of pent up emotion when a significant character undergoes a mental or physical change, often because of suffering, and must experience an emotional overflow." As the readers, we identify and empathize with the characters because suffering is a universal experience. However, by enduring our own catharsis—our powerful venting of emotion— we allow peace and balance to return to our own lives. In fact, Mr. Esta Powell, author of *Catharsis in Psychology and Beyond: A Historic Overview* says that people seek and enjoy ways to "symbolically relive their own painful emotional experiences and therefore achieve relief or resolution." One way we seek out these opportunities is through movies and books because, as Esta Powell says, "when personal distress is reawakened in a socially appropriate environment, such as theater, emotional experiences are not too overwhelming, because people are under the impression that they cry about the play character, but not about themselves."

We can experience the healing of catharsis by entering into Alexander's story. We connect with Alexander and the trouble he has getting ready in the morning because mornings are hard! We feel empathy in the trouble he has with his teacher and classmates. We enter deeper when we see that Alexander's dental work, shopping choices, and position in his family are painful. Our frustration and anxiety grow as we see Alexander near his breaking point several times. Even as he heads to bed, nothing is right. We're relieved when he puts his head down. We exhale our emotions and can hopefully rest peacefully knowing the value of a good-night's sleep to wash away the trials of the day.

Our catharsis is complete as we accept Alexander's mother's reminder that, "Some days are like that…" As we close the book, we have come full circle on our own trying day. With a glass of wine, we can unwind and leave Alexander and our day to rest.

Perhaps you can locate your old copy and read it aloud to the whole family at bedtime. It's amazing what a story like this one can do. Remember, everyone has days like that, even in Australia.

*Other books like this one:
Strega Nona by Tomie dePaola
Chrysanthemum by Kevin Henkes
The Day Jimmy's Boa Ate the Wash by Trinka Hakes Noble
Even Superheroes Have Bad Days by Shelly Becker

CHAPTER 2

Handling Anger

Where the Wild Things Are
by Maurice Sendak

———————

"A reader lives a thousand lives before he dies.
The man who never reads lives only one."
–George R.R. Martin

Maurice Sendak's work of timeless fantasy and art should be on all bookshelves! I used to keep this book on hand for my students. I taught high school English and yet so loved the cannon of children's literature that I kept a few books in my drawers for certain moods. Sometimes my students would walk into the classroom with heads down, grumbling about their exams. Other times they were fired up about a teacher who had wronged them or because so-and-so just didn't understand them. Those days I sensed that Max and his wolf suit were in order. I would climb up in my teacher chair—a director-style canvas and wooden chair with "Mrs. K" embroidered on it—hold up the book, and begin the day with the words, "The night Max wore his wolf suit…" As I read, I held up the book to show the class the pictures, just like an elementary school librarian would do. My sweet fifteen, sixteen, and seventeen-year-old students would listen intently, eyes glued to the pages. The child in each of us needs Max every now and again.

When we see Max's face with his visceral anger and hostility and pent-up frustration in his choice of costume and attitude, we can empathize. How many times have we wished we could actually act the way we feel or say what we really mean? Max yells to his mother, "I'll eat you up!" and can't we all just feel the irritation he expresses?

Americans seem angry. Turn on the TV and talk show hosts are arguing, listen to the radio and commentators are arguing, even professional athletes and the President are fighting. Road rage and revenge are very real dangers in many communities. It's also true that the constant suppression of our anger may be what causes more of it. Dr. James Averill, a psychology professor, was convinced that his academic colleagues misunderstood anger. Interviewed for Charles Duhigg's 2019 article in *The Atlantic*, Dr. James Averill said, "Everyone basically thought anger was something that mature people and societies ought to suppress." As a whole, we've accepted the idea that it is shameful to be an angry person. Even most professionals saw anger as a problem to be solved. However, Dr. Averill disagreed. Instead of becoming large blow-ups, these small episodes of anger tended to make bad situations better. Surprising even himself, Dr. Averill found that in "the vast majority of cases, expressing anger resulted in all parties becoming more willing to listen, to speak honestly," and more likely to accommodate one another's complaints. "People reported that they tended to be much happier after yelling at an offending party. They felt relieved, more optimistic, more energized." This is true for Max and for us as well.

When we give vent to our anger, we release our pent-up emotions and feel better. If we see Max as a role model in expressing anger without harm, we can begin to see a way for us to move through it rather than stuffing it in or, worse, exploding with it. Take a step back from your own anger and, with a few deep breaths, think about how to manage it like Max.

We use the phrase "blow off some steam." Do you need to let out some primal screams or growls? Do you need to find a punching bag, boxing ring, tough workout, or mountain to climb? Do you need your very own wolf suit?

Our need to process our anger in a safe way and in a safe space begins in our childhood. Maurice Sendak creates a way for us to see the powerful and transportive methods for processing emotions. When Max is sent to his room without supper, his mother is saying "no" to his poor choice in behavior and providing boundaries for Max to sort himself out. Most psychologists recommend establishing clear boundaries for children. Max's mother does this by sending him to his room where he can be a "wild thing." We, too, need safe spaces to let off some steam, to vent our frustrations. Perhaps that is with a trusted friend or spouse, maybe it's going for a run, or escaping with a good book. In Max's case, he can't physically escape or talk to someone else, but that doesn't stop him from healthily processing his anger.

Max's imagination is another healthy outlet for his anger. In his mind he can let his anger have full reign by imagining he is somewhere else. As a child can so easily do, Max escapes via his imagination to the land over the ocean. Maurice Sendak writes, "and an ocean tumbled by with a private boat for Max and he sailed off through night and day…" Through his imagination Max leaves the frustrating situation.

When we took the birthing classes at the hospital before our first child, Liesel, was born, the coaches told us to have some mental pictures in mind as "escapes" to focus on during the labor pains. My husband just had to say, "Remember Mendoza," and I was transported back to Argentina. I felt the cool air, the bright sunlight, the vast expanse of sky, the cobblestones, the smell of espresso, the patter of Spanish conversation, and I could forget I was in a hospital in excruciating pain. Our minds are powerful. This is an excellent way to process our problems. Max goes to his "happy place." Can you take this good advice? Run figuratively, but not actually?

Anger can also be managed by imagining we are someone else. Max imagines that he is someone else, someone with power, who is beloved and feared. Later in the story "[the wild things] were frightened and called him the most wild thing of all and made him king of all the wild things." Max currently holds no power in the real world. He is scolded for being too wild by his mother, who banishes him to his room. He can't refuse since she is the authority figure, despite what he might want to do, so he goes where he is in charge. Not only does he have power over himself and his choices and behaviors, but Max also has power over enormous untamed beasts! This is victory for Max.

What does this look like for grown-ups? "If I was in charge of _____, I'd do_____." Surely we've all had those conversations. Perhaps we've even attempted to find another job where we *can* be in charge. Or maybe, unhealthily so, we take it out on the people we do have power over. Maybe we vent our frustrations and feelings of being controlled by being overly controlling to our spouse or children or people who work under us. Max's solution seems a better road.

Finally, Max imagines that someone at home is missing him. He doesn't really want to stay mad or stay away. When we have spent our rage and energy, we often feel drained and depleted and empty. We see things as they are now instead of through an angry lens, and we need love and support. Returning feels hard and sad, painful even. We have to leave our world of "should be" and land in reality. We can't stay mad forever. We have to go back to work; we have to see them again. We have to let ourselves be loved again, like Max.

Max's return results in a loving mother's expectation that he'd be spent and hungry upon his return. She was right. And it didn't take Max as long as it might have seemed, for the dinner was still hot. For many of us, the anger may last longer, but we see that it doesn't have to.

We can return to our baseline with restored equilibrium, having given our inner wild-thing a chance to growl and rule and return.

*Other books like this one:
Jeremy Draws a Monster by Peter McCarty
Crankenstein by Samantha Berger
Llama Llama Mad at Mama by Anna Dewdney
The Grouchy Ladybug by Eric Carle
Maya was Grumpy by Courtney Pippin-Mathur

CHAPTER 3

Conquering Your Creativity Crisis

Harold and the Purple Crayon
by Crockett Johnson

"A book is a dream that you hold in your hand."

–Neil Gaiman

If you could draw the path of your future, where would it go? What would it look like? Do you believe that as adults we have the power to create our destiny? Asking these questions reflects our need to reconnect with our creative side. For most of us, creative expression seems like a luxury we can't afford or a skill we lack. Instead of dismissing our need for creativity, perhaps we should follow Harold's lead in Crockett Johnson's 1955 classic story and set off along the horizon, taking only what will help us create. We should leave armed with only what we need—a purple crayon.

In this book, Harold, a young boy, sets off on a nighttime adventure with only his trusty crayon. He has no idea where he is going, only that he set off in one direction and drew the path as he thought it up. He charts his own course complete with short-cuts, forked paths, and encounters with nature. He meets danger, solves tricky problems, and rescues himself from falling and drowning. Each time, his creativity saves him and eventually lands him safely at home.

Creativity, however, is not just something children have. In her book, *The Creativity Challenge,* Dr. KH Kim says, "Creativity doesn't decrease with age...[it] depends on the length of time they have been actively engaged in a field—not how old they are." But many of us have let our creative muscles atrophy. However, there are ways to reignite that part of us. After we decide to re-engage our creativity, we can see Harold as the mentor on our road back to innovation.

One of my favorite parts of this charming story is when Harold can't quite find his way home. He asks a policeman (the only adult in the landscape) who says nothing new or helpful and is in fact pointing the direction Harold was going anyway. As adults, we rely so heavily on paths outlined by "experts" rather than following writer Ralph Waldo Emerson's advice to "go where there is no path and leave a trail." Perhaps we are paralyzed by all the possibilities of the blank page in front of us. We don't know if our choice is the right one. We fail to be brave and forget that sometimes all we need is the purple crayon to change directions and to draw a different ending.

I recall a section in my elementary school library with books called *Choose Your Own Adventure*. The premises were always extraordinary, and the characters were brave and cunning. I wonder what changed between our free selves then and our conformist selves now? At what age do we stop feeling free to choose?

Maybe your muse is stifled or you are afraid of falling, like Harold does. So what do we do? How do we regain our creativity? Our "anything is possible" mentality? If we use Harold as our great example, we see that it requires blank space, diverse encounters, plenty of optimism, and endless curiosity. Dr. K.H. Kim suggests that, "having an independent attitude" is essential for creativity. That "although [innovators] learn from mentors, they remain free to choose what to do with their advice." In hope, I believe this freedom from others' constraint can be cultivated again.

Where is Harold at the end of the grand adventure he designed? Harold is tucked back in bed, just where he wanted to be. We live in such practical boxes. We are so afraid to mess up or stand out that we end up standing in the same spot with our purple crayon in hand, unused. Our cultural anxiety strangles us. We have a fascination with beige and gray in our home décor. As Henry David Thoreau said "The mass of men lead lives of quiet desperation." The collective of "social conformity" slowly kills us through paralysis and fear. Re-connecting with Harold can help us counteract this mentality.

One of my Pinterest boards pictures a sign that reads: "What if I fall?"
"My dear, what if you fly?"
Yes, what if? What if we face danger, plan an unexpected trip, build a house, start a business? What if we set out in a different direction from our parents? What if we get lost along the way? We might. We might also find a different view, a shortcut, a bit of beauty we wouldn't have seen elsewhere. Adventures are rarely smooth and safe. Even a small child like Harold knows this. At one point he draws

a monster to guard his beautiful, ripe, red apples, and the monster is so frightening it chases Harold away! And in his fear, he ends up in a boat on the ocean! This is more memorable than most of our lives all because he stepped out on a limb and took a risk with his purple crayon.

My practical mom would have made me take a pencil with an eraser instead of a colorful crayon. My husband would have chosen a mechanical pencil with extra lead. When I think about what I really, really feel like taking on my journey, I get a little frightened. What about you? Which would you choose?

If I was Harold and honest about what I really wanted, I would choose a big red marker. Permanent. Vibrant. Arresting. Wild. Do I have a permanent, vibrant, arresting, and wild life? Nope. But I am getting closer. The call of the blank page, rather than the color-by-number life, is in my head, in my ear, in my heart.

What else holds us back? Fear? Fear masquerading as practicality? When my husband and I built our house a few years ago, we ordered a stainless steel stove for our kitchen. The day our appliances were delivered, we removed the plastic and there was a stunning cherry red stove in my kitchen! I gasped and stood in front of it like I do at the Milwaukee Public Art Museum. The stove was a piece of art—more daring and intoxicating than I had dreamed for myself. I wish I could say we kept it. My husband and I looked at it and really liked it and walked around it and gazed at it, but our fear of making an expensive "forever choice" made us call the company back and remedy the order. Now we have a stainless steel stove with bright, shiny red knobs. I love the red, and I love the way it ties in with other red accents around my house—a daily reminder for me to take out my permanent red marker and enjoy a bit of adventure—but I wish we had kept it. It was beautiful and surprising and it might have helped me to dare daily.

We might not necessarily have anything in common with the character Harold, but maybe he's rather our child-ish hero. We long to go back to the way we were when life was easier and free of pressure and responsibility. What do you miss most about those days? Is it childlike hope? Wonder? A sense of possibility? At what point do we lose this freedom? What would it take for us to get back there?

If we're hoping to recapture our ability to be creative, to innovate, then Dr. K.H. Kim says we should spend lots of time "freethinking and playing alone...independen[ce] in solitude...entertain[ing oneself]...through pondering, writing, reading, etc..." It's just this sort of dreamy thinking that we need to kick-start in our lives again. In the past two years, I have tried to incorporate more of this in my own life. I sewed my first patchwork quilt, I read fiction on the couch, and work thousand piece puzzles on the dining room table. Carving out space to think and imagine does involve a spirit of adventure. To recapture our creativity we need to be willing to "venture into uncertain and risky creative endeavors…[to] jump on opportunities, and dare to explore," as Dr. K.H. Kim suggests.

We need to step out of the comfortable knowns of our lives and live more like Harold with excitement, not trepidation. Think about how that would look in your life right now. The worst that can happen might not be the worst after all. The risk of losing our creativity is greater than our fears of what others will think. Always remember nothing ventured, nothing gained. Take the first left and don't forget your purple crayon.

*Other books like this one:
Art & Max by David Weisner
Journey by Aaron Becker
Mina's White Canvas by Hyeon-Ju Lee
Not a Box by Antoinette Portis

CHAPTER 4

Our Need to Belong

Corduroy
by Don Freeman

———————

"Reading makes immigrants of us all. It takes
us away from home, but more important,
it finds homes for us everywhere."

–Jean Rhys

Don Freeman's 1968 children's classic begins with a small bear named Corduroy who sits on a department store shelf, hopeful of being chosen. One morning he is encouraged as a young girl picks him up; however, the girl's mother tells her she can't afford to buy the bear, plus there's a missing button on his overalls. Oh, what heartache! What a crushing blow to the little bear. Although Corduroy is deeply disappointed and suddenly disillusioned, he is determined to be worthy. Courageously, Corduroy takes his fate in his own hands and embarks on a mission to find his lost button. Along the way, he has more than a little adventure as Corduroy finds out when a mattress button flies off and he crashes into lamps creating a memorable mess in the department store at night. In his quest to be lovable, Corduroy goes to great lengths. He is wounded by being cast aside and unwanted when all he longed for was to belong.

If you've ever been looked-over, passed-over, last-picked, or left behind, you know the pain Corduroy feels. Longing to belong, Corduroy wishes to be taken home and loved best of all. For you and I, his story allows us to connect with that small child we still are inside, the one who wants to belong. Even as adults, we too, know that feeling. Sometimes we feel like the middle-schooler desperately waiting to be chosen for the team or silently longing to be asked to sit with the "cool kids." Perhaps we are the eager employee hearing the manager announcing a promotion and hoping we will be picked.

This loss of connection can make us feel desperate and depressed. Being told we're unloveable can feel like a sucker punch to the gut. If you are feeling this sense of disconnection, then this story has encouragement for you today.

If we're honest, we often respond to those moments of rejection just like Corduroy. We fixate on what is within our perceived control in order to remedy our failings. Is it our performance, something we said, something we missed, a previous experience, or none of these things? Sometimes it's not clear what caused our rejection. Maybe it's even something we can't help, but that is rarely a consolation.

I remember a particularly painful situation my freshman year of college. Late in the fall, dorm floors of all-boys began Roommate Roulette dates where each roommate calls up a date for his roomie, but it's a secret until the night of the date when she arrives. For several days, my friends had been receiving calls to go on these dates with various boys. One day I answered my dorm phone to find myself being asked out for just such a date. I was ecstatic! I felt like I belonged to the lovable group. I was one of the "cute girls." However, within 24 hours, the boy called me back to say that he had called "the wrong Maureen" and would be taking back his invitation. I was crushed. I know

now that there are greater tragedies and have walked with friends and family through painful divorces and losses, but I will never forget that feeling of dismissal.

So what's a girl, er, a bear to do when passed over? I recommend a little grief, a little emotional eating, but then, what if we begin to move forward? What if we strike out to find a solution? What if, as we seek to belong or seek to make ourselves more lovable, we actually find that we cannot retrieve our lost button? What will you and I do then? Maybe we rest awhile. Maybe we hide and pretend it's okay. These quests might be brutal. We might even fill it with attempts to get lost rather than found. Maybe we're even brought home by the authorities like Corduroy!

In the end of our search for belonging, we can hopefully say, "What an adventure!" Perhaps we discover that the skills we lack are not ones we really want to invest in anyway. Maybe we learn that the job we thought we wanted so badly wasn't the right fit for us after all. Maybe we realize we're worth waiting for. The goal is that in the end, even if we find ourselves right back where we started, we live now with acceptance.

Basic psychology says that much of human behavior, thought, and emotion stems from our psychological need to belong. Psychologist Marianna Pogosyan has studied the emotional consequences of belonging. She proposes that if bonding between people is a cause for happiness then "human beings could be wired to feel pain when we are bereft of social connection, just as [we] feel pain when we are deprived of our basic needs." We see this in the story of Corduroy. His very life feels incomplete without someone to love him. It's not just the way *he* feels. Belonging, Marianna Pogosyan says, "offers us the reassurance that we are not alone. We need others. For completing the patchwork of our identities, for the safety they give us to pursue our goals." We all have the need to belong.

At some point, we've all felt like we didn't belong. However, we can't stay defeated by the hurts of being rejected by someone. We need to release our anger or hurt and then come back to the start and put ourselves out there again. We need to come back around no matter how difficult the journey, like Corduroy, and accept that some people won't want us; they aren't our people. We need to prepare ourselves to try again.

When Corduroy's eyes open the next morning back on the department store shelf, he sees the very girl from the day before racing in to take him home. We also need to see that the right people will love us and accept us in spite of our perceived deficiencies. We will be loved and maybe even restored, like Corduroy, through the right relationship. His new friend, Lisa, takes Corduroy home. While she begins to sew a new button onto his overalls, she lovingly says, "I like you even without the button, but you'll be more comfortable this way." What an incredible gift to be accepted in spite of missing some things, but also to be loved enough to be restored. Are you willing to put yourself back out there again to risk rejection for belonging and hope for more?

We need to recognize the feeling, to see our hurt, but to move past it so that when belonging comes along again, we're ready, like Corduroy, waiting back on the shelf. Sometimes you have to step off the shelf and go after what you really want. Don't worry though. You aren't the only one longing to belong.

*Other books like this one:
Room for Bear by Ciara Gavin
Stellaluna by Janell Cannon
Otis by Loren Long
Fritz and the Beautiful Horses by Jan Brett

CHAPTER 5

Using Grit to Help Us Reach Our Goals

Mike Mulligan and His Steam Shovel
by Virginia Lee Burton

———————

"No book is really worth reading at the age of ten
which is not equally—and often far more—worth
reading at the age of fifty and beyond."
–C.S. Lewis

When you feel pushed out, used up, or outdated, almost nothing appeals more than quitting. In this classic book, Mike Mulligan and his steam shovel, lovingly named Mary Anne, have a legendary history filled with record-breaking feats of digging. They dug the foundations for the tallest buildings, cleared vast swaths of land for airports and dug through mountains for trains, but as technology changes, the steam shovels are out-paced. The jobs dry up and their spirits sag.

We can each identify with Mike and Mary Anne in some ways. Perhaps we have been phased out or grown too big for our previous roles. Initially, we may have been angry about the situation, which in turn becomes grief. When I left my teaching job to stay home with our daughter, it wasn't what I wanted to do. I wanted to return and applied for an extended leave. When that request was denied, I had to let go of my ideas about my career. It was very difficult. I identified so strongly as a teacher and struggled to accept my new identity. There were angry conversations with my husband and our families, lots of tears, and many sessions in therapy. I'd like to think I am not alone in dealing with this emotional transition. When have you felt passed over? Dried up? Did you wonder, "What's next?"

Like Mike and Mary Anne, we have two choices in these situations: we can fade out and quietly resign, ending up in the junkyard with the other steam shovels or we can, as Mike and Mary Anne do, look for different kind of work. We can go where others haven't been and find a new niche for ourselves. Mike and Mary Anne drive miles and miles to find work, gritty and united, until they come to the town of Popperville, where they heard there might possibly be a job. (Popperville's red town hall was modeled after the real one in West Newbury, Massachusetts and can still be seen today on Route 113.)

We can be encouraged by their persistence and their commitment to one another. When we feel left behind, do we exhibit the same drive? Angela Duckworth, psychology professor and researcher, calls this type of ambition "grit." "When considering individuals in identical circumstances, what each achieves depends on just two things, talent and effort. Talent—how fast we improve in skill—absolutely matters. But effort factors into the calculations twice, not once. Effort builds skill. At the very same time, effort makes skill productive." These are just the traits being studied for today's workplace and personal success.

"Grit is the new buzzword for success: at work, in school, in the gym. It's a combination of unshakable motivation, persistence, and determination. And the belief that improvement is always possible," according to Jane Clayson, reporter with wbur.org. Mike and Mary Anne had both talent and effort, they are an excellent example of grit. Although they knew they had what it takes to complete the job, they still needed to prove it to themselves as well as others in this new era of industrial changes.

Do we leave the people who might have gotten us this far, who have outlived their usefulness, by the side of the road as we move forward or do we loyally find something that will work for all of us? Mike finds a digging job, which seems small, but it matters to the people in Popperville. In this role, he and Mary Anne can do what they do best. We are encouraged by Mike's desire to tackle a new challenge. Mike is going to dig the basement for the town hall in a single day. Angela Duckworth calls this a "stretch goal, where one zeroes in on just one narrow aspect of their overall performance. Rather than focus on what they already do well, experts strive to improve specific weaknesses. They intentionally seek out challenges they can't yet meet." When Mike says that he will dig the basement in one day, he's setting a stretch goal, one he and Mary Anne had not yet accomplished. Grit is what keeps Mike and Mary Anne going.

Do we give up when the odds are against us, or do we work to improve so that we can stay in play? Think about your future. What stretch goal might you need to set and achieve in order to meet your larger goals? Also, ask yourself about your own grit. Do you have the same grit that Mike and Mary Anne had? Can you build up your grit?

We can also be encouraged by the town and its role in

the success of the operation. As Mike strikes a deal with the town supervisors to dig the foundation all in one day or the work is free, the crowds gather to see the outcome. The encouragement of the people helped Mike and Mary Anne to "dig a little faster and a little better." This is true for us, too! We all do better when we have people cheering us on. We know that a rallying crowd can fill us with adrenaline. The words of encouragement and the pressure can speed us to the finish.

Have you ever run a race? I ran a 5K or two myself—in another life and different body—and I always ran slower in practices than I did on race day. The cheering crowd, the signs and smiles and support made me push myself even harder. In *Grit*, Angela Duckworth interviews a retired mathematician, Rhonda Hughes, about her persistence and barrier-breaking. No one in Rhonda's family had ever been to college, and she really liked math more than stenography—the expected path for a woman. She eventually earned her PhD but received 79 rejection letters for applications to college faculty before being hired. For you and I, that might be too much resistance, too much difficulty to overcome. But Rhonda Hughes shares that it was the help of others cheering her on which allowed her to meet her goals. "There have been so many times in my career when I wanted to pack it in, when I wanted to give up and do something easier…but there was always someone who, in one way or another, told me to keep going. I think everyone needs somebody like that, don't you?"

The people of the nearby towns came to cheer for Mike and Mary Anne. The children from the school, the milkman, postman, traveling farmers, firemen, nearly everyone. As they worked while the crowd cheered, Mike and Mary Anne dug "a little better and a little faster." We, too, need someone to be our cheerleader, pushing us and helping us dig in. If you find meeting your goals nearly impossible, consider who is in your corner rooting for you. If you don't have that person yet, don't be afraid to ask someone.

While Mike Mulligan's story is good fiction, there are many other examples of great men and women whose grit made all the difference. One story I love is that of Brett Favre in 2003. Just one day after losing his father to a sudden heart attack, he led the Green Bay Packers to an incredible victory over the Oakland Raiders setting personal records and earning the admiration and love of all football fans. Despite being emotionally devastated, Brett Favre found an inner passion and determination to play and win the game for his father.

Mike's success benefitted more people than just himself. Because of his grit and success, the people he was working for gained more than they imagined. "Grittier people are more motivated to seek a meaningful, other-centered life…" says Angela Duckworth "If you take a moment to reflect on the times in your life when you've been at your best---when you've risen to the challenges before you, finding strength to do what might have seemed impossible—you'll realize that the goals you achieved were connected in some way, shape or form to the benefit of other people," she adds. Similarly, Mike Mulligan's perseverance is really what we *all* need. Call it grit, determination, stubbornness, a need to prove himself, or something else, this type of perseverance pays off. We need Mike to show us what is possible when we stick with our calling; when we refuse to be deterred.

The determined duo gets the new town hall's basement dug in one day, and, as it turns out, Mary Anne the steam shovel is stuck in the basement hole. In Mike and Mary Anne's haste to finish the job before the sun went down, they failed to make a way back out of the hole! Fortunately, the town allows her to become the furnace for the new town hall where she and Mike retire in comfort. The ending encapsulates what most of us want: to prove our mettle, to meet previously unmet goals, and to be rewarded for our achievement in ways that ultimately bring satisfaction to us.

As you turn the final page in Mike Mulligan, where do you find yourself? What are you close to giving up on? What do you feel discouraged about? What if you dug in and recommitted yourself to your calling? What if you saw yourself in Mike and Mary Anne and heard me and others cheering you on? A little better and little faster, you can do it!

*Other books like this one:
The Little Engine That Could by Watty Piper
Katy and the Big Snow by Virginia Lee Burton

CHAPTER 6

Getting Quality Sleep

Goodnight Moon
by Margaret Wise Brown

———————

"Some books are so familiar that reading
them is like being home again."
–Louisa May Alcott

"In the great green room there was a telephone and a red balloon." The opening line of this somnambulant picture book is etched into my head and heart like an epigram engraved in stone. With each of Margaret Wise Brown's phrases and pages, the audience sees a room of small, insignificant items in a child's nursery. However, as her central character says good night to each of them what Brown is doing for all of us is her greatest intention: lulling us to sleep.

As adults we need the message of *Goodnight Moon* as much, if not more, than our toddlers. We are a sleep-deprived country. Perhaps, if we listen to our friend Little Bunny, we will learn how to get the rest we need. The Sleep Foundation suggests that we structure our evenings intentionally for optimal sleep. We should consider the timing of our nighttime routine, the environment, and even what we eat before bed. Just like the character in the book, eating oatmeal as a bedtime snack is one of the best recommendations. The Sleep Foundation suggests that we "skip the white bread, refined pasta, and sugary baked goods, which may reduce serotonin levels and impair sleep. Instead, choose stick-to-your-ribs whole grains for your bedtime snack: popcorn, oatmeal, or whole-wheat crackers with nut butter are all good choices." Looks like that bowl of mush was a good and intentional choice for Little Bunny.

Two other aspects to retool include your bedtime routine and the sleeping environment. "Carve out at least 30 minutes of wind-down time before bed in which you do something relaxing, such as reading a book," The Sleep Foundation says. "While this might seem old-fashioned, the disruptions of our sleep systems by electronic devices is taking a toll. Dim the lights in the house slightly for an hour or so before bed, as the light from their screens can alert the brain and make it harder to fall asleep." Take your cues from the great green room; there are no electronics present. Similarly, we see the illustrations of the book grow darker as the words move from identification of objects to saying "Goodnight" to them, cuing Little Bunny and us.

"In order to calm your mind, do a breathing or relaxation exercise," The Sleep Foundation recommends. Shawn Stevenson, in his book *Sleep Smarter*, calls this practice mindfulness meditation. "Getting in and using your senses is a great way to practice mindfulness meditation. Mindfulness is really about noticing and tuning in to things in the here and now." "Good night kittens and goodnight mittens, good night bears and goodnight chairs." As we say goodnight to those things, we are walking ourselves into the freedom of sleep as Little Bunny and our little ones are, too. Like in *Goodnight Moon*, Little Bunny sees and senses the items around him in the bedroom. The light, the paintings on the walls, the sky. "What meditation truly does is give you the uncanny ability to focus. Meditation is a skill, a tool, and a necessity to help you relax," Shawn Stevenson says. Little Bunny's routine is relaxing for the reader as well.

The repetition of the word "goodnight" helps rock us, like the meter and rhythm of a rocking chair. The short phrases and repeated elements serve to lull us to sleep like a familiar melody. *Goodnight Moon's* predictability is reassuring, and as we drift off along with the little bunny, we might never realize what it is that calms us, but the cadence surely is intentional. If you are a mother, you know the slow rock of a mom with a babe in arms. I have been known to rock, even without a baby, in the pew at church, sitting silently. It's an unconscious rhythm and it lulls me into a near slumber, day or night. Margaret Wise Brown's lullaby is just what we need.

Maybe your version of *Goodnight Moon* goes something like this; in my small, cluttered, cream-painted bedroom/office there is a pile of laundry (uncertain of its status), a stack of things I've meant to read, a hamper that my husband's socks never make their way into, a ceiling fan that wobbles on high, and a squeaky closet door. In my room, there is no old lady whispering "hush," only me when my husband snores. Shhhhhhh, I say. There is a cell phone with notifications and a tiny light signaling "charging." There is no clock (that's what my phone is for). Compared to the sleeping bunny at the end of this book, I am much too stimulated to sleep well. Perhaps we should consider some old school habits for sleep health. Little Bunny has both an old school phone and an old school clock in his room.

Little Bunny also falls asleep with a reassuring presence in his room. I don't know about you but when my husband travels or is out late, I have trouble going to sleep. While I luxuriate in the extra space (I'm a diagonal, spread-eagle sleeper when left alone), I never really feel as secure as when he is home. The little old woman rocking and knitting and whispering "hush" is Little Bunny's reassuring security. There is a reason our kids like to climb into our beds in the middle of the night and why they ask us to cuddle longer in theirs when we put them to sleep. It feels good and snuggly to have someone you love, who is warm and gentle, wrapping their arms around you and bringing their peace to you.

A favorite childhood image that comes to mind is the scene from the original *Mary Poppins* movie, the one where the Banks children have been out in the park having adventures with Mary Poppins and Bert and are now exhausted yet wide-eyed with memories of all they did that day. They claim they cannot go to sleep, so Mary Poppins sits and darns a sock and rocks and sings and they peacefully drift off to sleep. She sings this lovely, haunting song called "Stay Awake." That lullaby nearly puts me to sleep every time I hear it. Her presence provides reassurance, and her song is just the right cadence.

Then, almost so subtly you'd miss it, Little Bunny is crawling towards the covers. He begins in position on the bed and as the recitation of "Goodnights" continues, he moves closer and closer to under the covers. Goodnight everything…except my mind, my worries, my phone… Yes, *Goodnight Moon* is very much for us now. So tonight, turn off, unwind, breathe deeply, and rest. "Goodnight stars, goodnight air, goodnight noises everywhere."

*Other books like this one:

Goodnight, Goodnight Construction Site by Sherri Duskey Rinker
The World Champion of Staying Awake by Sean Taylor

CHAPTER 7

Standing Up to Shame

Ira Sleeps Over
by Bernard Waber

———————

"Once you have read a book you care about,
some part of it is always with you."
–Louis L'Amour

Like all of the stories in this book, this one appears to be about a young boy and his first sleepover, but it's also about much more. At the start of the story Ira is so excited to sleep at his friend Reggie's house. His older and (supposedly) wiser sister pokes holes in Ira's self-confidence as she asks, "What about Teddy?" While Ira had originally planned to take his beloved teddy bear, he now hesitates because of his sister's comments. His insecurity wins, convincing him that his friend would make fun of him. In the end, Ira discovers that his friend also has a security toy and their friendship is strengthened by sharing this moment.

Bernard Waber's 1972 classic children's book shows us that people, even people we love, can suggest a way of being that is not authentic to our true selves. While she may be aware of what she's doing, Ira's sister may not realize the depth of the wound she causes. None of the things that Ira is feeling are abnormal, but his sister makes him doubt himself. She suggests that he is unlike other boys his age, and she makes him feel self-conscious and alone. Rather than encourage Ira, she assures him that his friend will laugh at him. "And did you think about how he will laugh and say, 'Tah Tah' is a silly, baby name, even for a teddy bear?" Ultimately, Ira decides not to take the (very age-appropriate) thing that makes him feel safe and strong in unfamiliar settings.

We, too, often begin our adventures with excitement. Many of us, especially as young children, launch ourselves into new experiences without over-thinking them. All it takes, though, is one detractor (in this case a big sister) to call our attention to our fears and insecurities. These people cast shame on us for being who we are. Ira is young and nervous about doing something new. Ira's sister brings up feelings of shame and insecurity in Ira for his coping methods. For us, too, certain situations may lead to feelings of shame in our personal or professional arenas. Shame researcher Brené Brown defines shame as "the feeling that washes over us and makes us feel so flawed that we question whether we're worthy of love, belonging, and connection." What Ira fears, then, is feeling disconnected from his friend, Reggie.

"Our ego will do almost anything to avoid or minimize the discomfort associated with feeling vulnerable...because it's too risky. *What will people think? What if I learn something unpleasant or uncomfortable about myself?*" Brené Brown says. That means we, too, can be like Ira. We can become afraid of bringing our true self or the things that make us feel secure, whether they are tangible or intangible, into our grown-up situations. Instead of being true to who we are and what we need, we can be misled by others to believe that those needs are silly, immature, or abnormal. When that happens, we tend to respond like Ira—we waffle, we obsess, we worry, we try to feel the situation out the way Ira asks, "What do you think about teddy bears?" without giving away our secret.

Have you felt pressured to leave your "teddy bear" at home, whatever that means to you, even when it would have helped you show up as a better version of yourself? Was it because of something someone said or because of a fear that others might laugh at you? What is that thing? Is it your devotion to your family? Is it dressing differently than others?

For me, it was getting a tattoo. I grew up in a conservative home and church. The messages I internalized included that tattoos were against the Bible and a part of a deeper, evil sub-culture. However, at age 36, after three long, hard years of depression, including a suicide attempt, I emerged a different person. The feeling of coming back from a figurative death made me want to memorialize it, to remember where I was and what I had been through. A tattoo felt right. But that would mean doing something risky. And my husband was not a big fan. I waffled. I worried. I tabled it.

And then, once I sat with some of the thoughts others had placed in me, I realized that they were shame-inducing and simply not true. So I took my brave friend, or rather I made her take me, and I got the tattoo. I have the words "Never Once" written on the inside of my forearm. This reminds me, whenever I look at it, that I was never alone during that dark season and that God never forgot me. And rather than shame, it fills me with hope that I know I will be okay. People ask about it often and the story is an encouragement to anyone who hears it. If I had listened to the voices of others, I would still be wondering what it would be like, and I would still be conforming to the image they expected. I am so glad I chose to follow my own voice. I am more myself when I take with me the things that make me feel secure and confident.

Ira's sister expected Reggie to laugh, and she expected Ira to feel foolish. As a mean big sister, she wanted him to feel those things. But in the end, Ira realizes that he is more like his friend Reggie than he had ever thought possible. They were both trying to hide the same insecurity! "When someone feels sorry for us, it magnifies our feelings of being alone. When someone feels with us, it magnifies our feelings of connection and normalcy," Brené Brown says. Think about what time would have been saved, what discomfort avoided, if they had both just brought their authentic selves from the very beginning.

Along with shame and connection comes vulnerability. In her most recent book, *Dare to Lead,* Brené Brown describes vulnerability as "the birthplace of love, belonging and joy." This is precisely what Ira and his friend Reggie have between them, and the desire to have a sleepover is evidence that they are both longing for an even deeper connection. Their friendship brings them great joy. While fear and shame threaten to disconnect them, the book has a happier ending.

When you close the cover on Ira's story, I hope that you feel empowered to be the real you; to ignore the voices that make you feel shame for what you are hiding. Secrets lose their shame when they are brought to light. Then bravely inspect your own life for places you may be shaming yourself or others. Ask yourself, what about my role as a parent? Do I try to "spare" my children any perceived ideas that they will be shamed for something that makes them who they are? Do I unintentionally impose my own fears on them; wordlessly telling them it's not okay to be themselves? That they should hide what others wouldn't like about them if they really knew? What might be different if we saw the strength and similarity in this story?

Ira's advice for us: don't hide yourself, take all of you into every situation.

*Other books like this:

Galimoto by Karen Lynn Williams

Three Bears in a Boat by David Soman

Ish by Peter H. Reynolds

CHAPTER 8

Risk

Bread and Jam for Frances
by Russell Hoban

———————

"If one cannot enjoy reading a book over and over again,
there is no use in reading it at all."

–Oscar Wilde

As a carbivore (one who only eats carbs), I completely identify with the character Frances the badger who eats bread and jam for every meal. Even though her parents try to get her to eat other things, like veal chops and green beans, she only wants bread and jam. "She won't try anything new," her mother tells her father.

Frances explains, "There are many different things to eat, and they taste many different ways, but when I have bread and jam I always know what I am getting and I am always pleased."

In Russell Hoban's 1964 book, Frances is like many of us: happily in control and confidently predictable. Despite the fact that her parents were perfectly willing to offer Frances food prepared different ways, perhaps in more appealing ways, she has an excuse for why all of them (eggs in particular) are bad. Eventually, her parents stop offering her other options, and Frances starts to realize that she is missing out. She chooses to take a risk by trying a bite of spaghetti. Ultimately, she finds that the risk was worth the flavorful reward.

Do you have a response every time someone asks you to try something new or take a smallish risk? Do you have all the angles covered? Do your eggs, like Frances', "fall off the fork and roll under the table?" If so, then you could probably learn a lot from Frances.

Risk-takers show us that we do miss out when

we stay the way we've always been. I wonder what we might discover if we opened ourselves up to a new food, experience, person, song, skill, or place. Like many people, I can relate to Frances. There were many foods I didn't try until I was almost thirty. I had never tried seafood, pad Thai, curry, feta cheese, dates, Brussels sprouts, or anything interesting, really. I didn't think about it much either. Like Frances, my practical, pleasure-seeking-self believed that knowing exactly what I liked ensured a lovely experience. But, like Frances, it did get boring, especially when I saw other people enjoying various exotic meals. Now that I know better, we have a new rule at our house. Everyone has to have a "no thank you" bite. This is how I get my kids to try new things. How will they ever know what they might like if they never try even a bite?

What is risk, and why is it worth taking? Or maybe you are wondering what is an appropriate risk to take? "Risk is a decision or behavior that has a significant probability of resulting in a negative outcome," extreme free-solo rock climber Kayt Sukel says in her book, *The Art of Risk*. Sounds rather unwise, doesn't it? She goes on to say that "positive or negative, specific or broad, general or personal, the one thing all definitions of risk have in common is the idea of uncertainty." That sounds rather unsettling for those of us who like predictability. Most people would describe risk as something best to avoid.

How do you calculate risk? How do your emotions and past experiences affect your willingness to take risks? When looking at Frances' aversion to risk and her security tied to the certain enjoyment of a jelly sandwich, where do you see yourself?

Humans like certainty. It makes us feel in control and safe. But sometimes certainty traps us. Frances' mother encouraged her to try new things, and yet she remained stubborn and stuck. Do we know we're stuck? Frances' mother counters her efforts to dodge trying a new dinner. She reminds Frances that she "tries new things in her school lunches." Then Frances confesses that every day she trades away her lunch for bread and jam.

Frances' very clever parents decide to only offer bread and jam for breakfast, lunch, and dinner. This becomes disappointing for Frances, especially when compared with her school-friend, Albert who always has a variety of foods in his lunch. She also feels left out among her family when they all enjoy spaghetti and meatballs, and her plate contains only bread and jam. Since she never tries anything new, her family thinks she never *will* like something else. She eventually realizes the bread and jam is a prison of her own making. Frances doesn't like the way that feels.

Does our rut ever seem confining? Do we ever wish we could be like so-and-so who does_____? What stops us? Uncertainty over where to begin, perhaps? Kayt Sukal would say assess, practice small risks, and then push ourselves to take the bigger risk.

Some of us are more predisposed to taking risks. "Our genes, our neurochemicals, and our brain circuitry," says Kayt Sukel all affect our response to risk taking. Despite some aspects of our nature we can't control, there are some we can. Many of the risk-taking factors within our control "can include your familiarity with a situation, your social group, your emotional response, your stress level, and your response to failure," Kayt Sukel discovered. This is great news for those of us who are more reserved and even fearful. But these factors also hold true, "for those who are naturally inclined to push the envelope," Kayt Sukel says.

One particularly interesting aspect of growing our risk-taking behavior is that the evidence reveals that "the more people you know who are engaging in a particular activity, the more likely you are willing to engage in it too. And that's even if you don't think it's actually a good thing to do," finds Kayt Sukel. So if you want to build up your risk-taking muscle, train with those who take risks. I think our parents called it "peer-pressure," but remember not all peer-pressure is bad. Frances' friends at school had very fancy, interesting, and varied lunches. Her plain one started to feel just that—plain. The positive pressure of her peers was part of what propelled her to take a risk. Are you surrounded by people who challenge you or who think exactly like you? What would it take for you to step out? If we never try, we'll never know.

When Frances takes a risk with spaghetti and meatballs, she realizes she likes it, and she eats up every bite. The risk-reward ratio was small but meaningful. Gaining confidence after that risk, Frances takes a bigger risk with her school lunch and finds that it is indeed delicious to take risks. When we part ways with Frances, she is enjoying tomato soup, a lobster-salad sandwich, celery, carrot sticks, black olives, a little salt shaker for the celery, two plums, and a tiny basket of cherries with vanilla pudding and chocolate sprinkles all placed on top of a lace doily with a vase of violets nearby. Her friend Albert notices that it's a good lunch. And Frances finally declares, "I think it's nice that there are all different kinds of lunches and breakfasts and dinners and snacks."

Some risks have even greater rewards. In college, my boyfriend and I went to different schools, separated by over 400 miles. Many of you know long-distance relationships are difficult, and so I took a big risk by transferring from my school to his. I left a place I knew, with friends and professors who knew me, to join him on a campus I had never officially toured, where I knew only a handful of people. It was terrifying and a serious adjustment. By grace, it worked out well in the end. He's now my husband of nearly 18 years and the risk was definitely worth the reward.

It's worthwhile to evaluate where we are right now and where we would like to be someday. Remember, exercising that risk-taking muscle strengthens your confidence to take the next risk. And it's always helpful to ask, what's the worst that could happen? As you ramp up to taking greater risks, the rewards grow, too. I feel confident that the lessons we learn when we risk are invaluable and often far better than we can imagine.

*Other books like this one:
Green Eggs and Ham by Dr. Seuss
Chester's Way by Kevin Henkes

CHAPTER 9

People-pleasing

The Seven Silly Eaters
by Mary Ann Hoberman

———————

"You know you've read a good book when you turn the
last page and feel a little as if you have lost a friend."

–Paul Sweeney

"Creamy oatmeal, pots of it! Homemade bread and lots of it! Peeling apples by the peck, Mrs. Peters was a wreck!" These exclamations are the final straw for one very exhausted woman in Mary Ann Hoberman's tale of a mother catering to her children's very narrow food requests. The delightful rhyming belies a message that plagues many of us as adults, and not just with pleasing our children. Mrs. Peters, the story says, spends her days preparing what they each prefer. She works to meet the demands of each child while attempting to manage the rest of their very full home. She begins alright despite children throwing milk on the floor, or spitting it out, or refusing it altogether; despite them screaming that the lemonade was not homemade; despite lumpy oatmeal being spilled on the cat and more. Her patience and willingness to continue seems exhausting to the point of lunacy!

Who do we keep catering to despite the near madness of it all? Who are we afraid of upsetting? Our boss, perhaps? Yes, I'll stay late again. Yes, I'll work this weekend. Yes, I'll get that report done right now. Yes, yes, yes. Or our kids' activities? Yes, school PTA. Yes, room parents. Yes, children's ministry. Yes, neighborhood association. Alma mater. Old lady next door. Mother-in-law. Yes, yes, yes! Until one day we snap! Or break down, or fall into bed unable to get out.

We all know the saying "you can't please all of the people all of the time," but how many of us actually live that way?

I would argue that we are so afraid of letting anyone down that we neglect to care for ourselves. Women and mothers are most often prone to this. As nurturers and caretakers, we want to help. As women who want to be seen as capable, we refuse to say no. And we end up like Mrs. Peters.

"People-pleasers whose disease to please is predominantly caused by habitual behavior are driven to take care of others' needs at the expense of their own…[they] do too much, too often for others, almost never say, 'no,' rarely delegate, and inevitably become overcommitted and spread too thin," Psychologist and researcher Harriet B. Braiker, in her book *The Disease to Please,* writes. This describes poor Mrs. Peters to a tee! I would say this probably describes many of us as well. If you need more straight-talk about this tendency, again, Harriet B. Braiker says, "The truth is that 'people-pleasing' is a sweet-sounding name for what, to many people actually is a serious psychological problem!"

[Mrs. Peters] "wiped her brow and heaved a sigh, another year was passing by. In fact, she realized with sorrow, her birthday would arrive tomorrow! Drearily she shook her head and wearily went up to bed," Mary Ann Hoberman says. I don't know about you but I sure have felt this way—utterly spent from the demands of taking care of all the people and all the things that come to me. Was it up to me to keep it all together? The weight of others' expectations will beat us if we aren't careful. "Your conscience will orient you to the expectations of others. By your demonstrated willingness to put others' needs before your own, you continue to accord other people a position of authority over you. Even though you may be taking care of others in what feels like a parental capacity, and meeting your adult obligations and responsibilities, your conscience still treats you like an obedient or disobedient child," Harriet B. Braiker explains.

We've got to stop and evaluate our situations. For a mother of young children, there may be times when caretaking is required, but we need to be wary of the ways that our care can turn into a vicious cycle. We must treat ourselves more kindly. "Holding yourself to perfectionist standards [like those of Mrs. Peters] is nothing short of self-imposed emotional cruelty," Harriet B. Braiker determines. When people ask how we are we say, "busy, busy!" At what expense are we living this way? Maybe it's fear. What if we let people down? What if we couldn't do all that people ask of us? Assume for a moment that we do let people down or we can't do all the things. What's the worst that could happen? I remember one of my first counseling appointments with a new psychologist. I told him all the things I was doing/responsible for. He just looked shocked and then said, "No wonder you're here!" Clearly, I needed to wake-up!

When put like that, perhaps we can finally see our peril. One way is to realize that if we hope to do less for others (such as the things they can easily do for themselves) then we need to tell them. Do you make coffee every morning for the entire office? What if you didn't make it one morning? Do you cater to ungrateful co-workers, day in and day out? These questions are worth asking yourself.

If your answer is that you must continue to do these things lest others label you selfish, then listen up. This is not true! While children are young or parents are very aged, caring for oneself can feel like a selfish choice, but that is an unhealthy attitude. Their care is only as healthy as the caregiver. In fact, "people-pleasers train themselves to deny their own needs while, at the same time, they inadvertently teach others not to take care of them either," Harriet B. Braiker says. Our competence works against us; the more we do, the more we are expected to do. The outcome of this cycle is we are depleted, exhausted, discouraged, depressed and probably crying.

If this sounds like you, then Mrs. Peters' response is for you. Go to bed. And then in the morning find some boundaries, and stick to them. Make everyone pitch in. Delegating responsibilities gives others a share of the stress and also allows the others to have a share in the outcome. The brunt of the work no longer relies solely on you! Stop doing for others what they can do for themselves.

In Hoberman's story, the precious children sense their mother is due some recognition. And in their very helpless way, the children attempt to serve their mother.

In the middle of the night, the children attempt to cook for their mother all the things she does for them. Even in their failures, their attempt to help themselves and serve her spectacularly succeeds in the form of a cake that makes everyone happy. "And from that day to this, 'tis said, The Peters family all is fed a single simple meal—just one—a meal that's good for everyone. They all take turns in mixing it, they all take turns in fixing it. It's fine to eat and fun to make—it's Mrs. Peters' birthday cake."

And in the end, we can see that Mrs. Peters finally drew some boundary lines. She stopped cooking for all of their peculiarities and made them all help share the load. These are such healthy responses that we too, as people-pleasers, can benefit from implementing. Stop enabling bad habits and teach responsibility and a team approach.

When we do everything to keep everyone else happy, we fail to make ourselves happy. But when we allow other people to do things for themselves, even if they fail, we're all happier (and saner). We lower our collective expectations and share the burden, resulting in a closer community. It will probably be messy and flawed, but certainly worthwhile.

*Other books like this one:
Noni Says No by Heather Hartt-Sussman
Me, Me, Me by Annika Dunklee and Lori Joy Smith
The Giving Tree by Shel Silverstein

CHAPTER 10

Empathy in Grief and Loss

The Tub People
by Pam Conrad

"Reading is the sole means by which we slip, involuntarily, often helplessly, into another's skin, another's voice, another's soul."

–Joyce Carol Oates

I stumbled upon this story in a wonderful anthology of children's literature after my oldest child was born. In this poignant tale of a family of bathtub toy characters, Pam Conrad describes a beautifully predictable childhood. The little tub child plays, the family spends time together, the grown-ups enjoy one another's company, and they have delightfully repetitive days in the bath. At that point in the story, we are all recalling how we spent hours in the baths ourselves as children. We scooped and poured, held our breath in contests, made silly hairdos, and raced our wind-up boats. We played very much like the story's central character, the Tub Child, does. In this fairly mundane setting, the rituals of the bath, both for us and the characters, lull us toward complacency. We, like children, can believe that things will always stay this way. Just the way we like them, expect them, enjoy them.

But then, like real life, things change in an instant. Suddenly, "one evening the bathwater began rushing down the drain before they were all lined up [along the edge of the bathtub as usual], pulling all the Tub People this way and that...and the Tub Child disappeared down the drain without a sound." What a disastrous scenario for the family!

The next page just wrecks me. The picture is of the Tub Mother with her face and body laying over the top of the tub drain. "The Tub Mother pressed her face to the grating.

She looked and looked for her Tub Child. But she could not see him."

The first time I read this story I had an immediate distaste. The horror! The agony! What a terrible story for children! And for mothers! The loss Tub Mother must feel for her child!

As a parent, being completely unable to save your child must be the worst feeling of all. The emotions one feels upon such a devastating, blinding loss are enormous. Just the thought of any of the horrible things that could happen to my children twists me into a knot of anxiety. Of course, these thoughts are not productive as they hinder my ability to mother my children and live my life. A place of constant "what if" is no place to live.

I think the reason I disliked this book the first few times through was that when the Tub Child is sucked into the drain, it feels like a gut punch. As a mother, I can literally feel the tug on my insides. This is the truth in this story; no one sees trouble coming. If we could prepare adequately, it might not hurt so much, but we can't prepare for real life. That is why I think *The Tub People* is just the right story to help one develop empathy for grief and loss. By connecting with this story, I dip my toe in the vast ocean of grief without being swept away by it.

Roman Krznaric, author of the book, *Empathy,* defines empathy as "The art of stepping imaginatively into the shoes of another person, understanding their feelings and perspectives, and using that understanding to guide your actions." The topic of loss may seem too dark or deep for children, but research indicates that children have an incredible capacity for empathy. This is one reason why this book is such an excellent choice for children. Yet the value of this story is not just for children. Humanity needs greater empathy. According to Roman Krznaric, "Political and ethnic violence, religious intolerance, poverty and hunger, human rights abuses, global warming—there is an urgent need to harness the power of empathy to tackle these crises and bridge social divides. This requires thinking about empathy not just as a relationship between individuals… but as a collective force that can shift the contours of the social and political landscape." If we worked to gain collective empathy rather than popularity, I wonder what positive changes would result.

So I exercise my empathy muscles as I sit with the Tub Family while the washcloth makes a "lonely dripping sound," and they feel "very sad." Pam Conrad describes how the other Tub People set out to look for their child and how they called for him, even though they knew where he had gone. "Every evening the Tub People continued to float in the bathwater…but in time they stopped calling… and they never winked at each other anymore." Oh, my heart hurts for them!

When I read this book, and my heart feels for the mother and her entire family, I have begun this hard work of empathizing. "There is nothing like looking through someone else's eyes to help question your own assumptions and prejudices and spark new ways of thinking about your priorities in life...Ultimately, the best reason to develop the habit of empathizing is that empathy can create the human bonds that make life worth living," Roman Krznaric says in *Empathy*. The goal then is to apply this practice to the rest of my life. That I would, as a result, become a more empathic person in the "real world" where I live each day. That I would see others, truly see them, as common humanity. That I would be equally empathic across all aspects of my life. That what I read, see, and experience would all receive my care. These are lofty goals but for such a worthy cause!

The best thing about this book is that Tub Child does come home. After the water drains slower and slower and the plumber is called to come and fix that "terrible drain," the Tub Child is pulled out, "wet and tired." And with too much time in the middle, the family waits for word and reunification. Waiting is hard. Waiting with hope can be excruciating. We, too, enter in to their grief and feelings of loss. We, too, hold our breath and wait for his safe return. But since we don't yet know the outcome, our ability to rest and believe in miracles hinges on his return. We experience all the feels, all the catharsis, without hopefully ever having to lose our own child down a drain.

My own mother once lost my sister. While the two were separated for only a few minutes, my mother recalls the deep agony of not knowing where Megan was. My mom says she was beside herself and coming unglued as she looked throughout the department store, calling Megan's name, moving faster and faster among the aisles of clothing. She was certain that my sister had been snatched by a stranger in seconds. The feeling of loss and panic gripped my mother much like it did Tub Mother. And mercifully, both stories had happy endings.

Then "finally…they were lifted up and carefully carried into a new room and gently placed on a large, soft bed!" Finally, all seven of the Tub People are together again! The Tub Child has been returned, and their family is whole once more. The joy of being together overshadows their relocation out of the water and into unfamiliar territory in a bedroom. What they lost in location and familiarity, they received back in the salvation of their child.

While we enter into this story and can walk the path of grief and loss, we are not left in despair at the conclusion. For children and for us, it gives us a place to gain empathy and to recognize the fragility of life. The fleeting moments of joy are to be celebrated and enjoyed because they are not guaranteed. Maybe today you need to speak your gratitude aloud. Maybe you need to call a friend who has experienced deep grief and put your new empathy lessons into practice. And maybe, go hug all of your people a little bit tighter tonight.

*Other books like this one:
The Invisible Boy by Trudy Ludwig
The Hundred Dresses by Eleanor Estes
Amazing Grace by Mary Hoffman

CHAPTER 11

Appreciation

Last Stop on Market Street
by Matt de la Peña

———————

"In the case of good books, the point is not to
see how many of them you can get through,
but how many can get through to you."

–Mortimer Adler

The talented author, Matt de la Peña, draws our attention to some of the little things we take for granted each day as we ride along with CJ and his Nana on the bus towards their weekly service at the soup kitchen in his poignant book, *Last Stop on Market Street*. When was the last time you smelled the air or noticed how the rain looked? Through CJ's eyes, I notice the way I look at little things, mostly with a negative or annoyed lens. "The outside air smelled like freedom, but it also smelled like rain, which freckled CJ's shirt and dripped down his nose." When CJ complains about the rain, his Nana tries to help him see the beauty and wonder of the ordinary. "Trees get thirsty, too," his Nana told him. Don't you see that big one drinking through a straw?" And even though her grandson doesn't yet have eyes to see the beauty, she is undeterred.

When CJ complains about riding the bus and not having a car like his friends' families do, Nana draws his attention to the variety of people on their bus and the ways in which they enrich her life and his. She consistently returns his negative thoughts about the bus with vivid sensory reminders, always focusing on the people. When CJ complains about what he sees that he doesn't have, she redirects him. As the story goes on he imitates his grandmother as she closes her eyes to listen to the music being played by a man with a guitar. It's then that his mind sees and feels something deeper, and his senses overwhelm his soul with magic.

Have you ever closed your eyes and used all five senses to take in the beauty around you? The next time you watch a sunset or sit along the banks of the creek under the canopy of trees, be mindful of the little ways the magic of noticing can change your mood.

I love how this book ends. The last stop on Market Street is a neighborhood no one would travel to by choice. It's crumbling and broken-down, with "graffiti-tagged windows and boarded-up stores." When CJ wonders why the area is in shambles his Nana reminds him that "sometimes when you're surrounded by dirt, you're a better witness for what's beautiful."

CJ's Nana had profound insights about everyday occurrences that CJ himself couldn't yet see, perhaps because of his age or perhaps because the eyes of his soul had not yet been opened. In his book, *Seeing What Others Don't,* Gary Klein writes that insights are shifts, "like discontinuous discoveries—unexpected transitions from a mediocre story to a better one." Throughout this fascinating book, Gary Klein demonstrates that these new ways of seeing change us for the better. For starters, these discoveries give us new perspectives. When you begin to see, what new story might you tell?

Along with CJ, we, too, see the beauty all around the

soup kitchen at the end of the story. In places where our former stories told us about a run-down neighborhood or about not having the things others do, the new story, with its new insights, opens our minds and senses, allowing us to see the world as a beautiful musical painting, ultimately transforming CJ and us, if we let it.

"Appreciating the meaningful things and people in our lives may play an even larger role in our overall happiness than previously thought," says Stacey Kelley in her article about studying happiness. The students surveyed in the study were asked to measure their levels of appreciation, defined as "acknowledging the value and meaning of something—an event, a behavior, an object—and feeling positive emotional connection to it." Then appreciation is a transformed way of looking at ordinary things.

The study's results also suggest that "appreciation is twice as significant as gratitude in determining overall satisfaction with life." While appreciation is seeing value and meaning in ordinary things, a transformed way of thinking, gratitude is different. Gratitude is acknowledgment, thankfulness for what you have. For you and I to begin to practice this appreciation, we need to start to see life like CJ's Nana. We need to "focus on and value what [we] have, spend time outdoors, and reflect on [our] blessings and relationships with others."

This fall I began volunteering at an inner-city elementary

school. The drive to this school takes me through areas of town that are boarded up, vacant, broken-down and depressing. Trash litters the streets, the yards are uncared for, and the homes are nearly condemned. It's hard to feel positive in a place like that. Yet, each time I walk into the doors at St. Marcus School, I see beauty and light all around me. The children's faces are smiling and they generously give hugs. As I sit and work with them on reading, they beam under praise—all of them want to be chosen to work with me. I see beauty in a neighborhood that looks ugly. It's been a lesson for me in appreciating small things and looking for the beauty no matter where I am.

Because of his Nana's true vision, CJ begins to see things she does in places "where he never even thought to look." What if you and I look around us again, or even travel to where things look a little worn and practice seeing, really seeing, the beauty and the people like CJ's Nana sees them. Maybe, like Louis Armstrong sings in his song, "What a Wonderful World," we'd see "skies of blue, clouds of white and think to ourselves what a wonderful world…" Maybe it would transform more than just our minds.

*Other books like this one:
Blackout by John Rocco
The Snowy Day by Ezra Jack Keats
Tomorrow Most Likely by David Eggers

CHAPTER 12

Friendship

Officer Buckle and Gloria
by Peggy Rathmann

———————

"There is no friend as loyal as a book."
–Ernest Hemingway

Officer Buckle is the kind of guest speaker and safety guru that easily tires his audience. His droll delivery and endless rules make our eyes roll back in our heads, quickly induce sleep, and can take the fun right out of childhood. At the start of the story, the children regularly fall asleep during Officer Buckle's safety presentations. The staff and students alike disregard general safety as they've never really learned anything from these snooze-worthy seminars.

While the content of his messages was important and relevant, his delivery needed help. As we look across the audience, we see kids doodling, throwing paper airplanes, and turning around backwards. "Sometimes, there was [even] snoring." In all fairness to Officer Buckle, the town is called, Napville! Still, his annual safety presentations definitely needed an entertaining boost. Enter: Gloria.

One day, Officer Buckle gets a new police dog named Gloria, and he brings her along to his next Safety Speech. He tells the children about her and demonstrates her obedience. When the speech begins, Officer Buckle believes Gloria is doing the last thing he commanded her to do: sit.

To his surprise, the kids and teachers in the audience are laughing and paying attention! They are roaring and cheering and clapping their hands. What he doesn't realize is that Gloria is acting out all of the safety tips behind his back! When he sees the audience's enthusiastic response,

Officer Buckle is encouraged to make his speech more engaging. "Officer Buckle grinned. He said the rest of the tips with *plenty* of expression…Officer Buckle was surprised. He had never noticed how funny safety tips could be," Peggy Rathmann writes.

After the speech, Officer Buckle received many letters of thanks. His favorite letter said "You and Gloria make a good team." This was the message. These two were a perfect combination. The requests for Officer Buckle's safety speech came rolling in. Everyone wanted him to come and share, always with Gloria, too. Everywhere they went, "the children sat up and listened." And "after every speech, Officer Buckle took Gloria out for ice cream. Officer Buckle loved having a buddy." Again! This is the message of the story—the message you and I need to hear.

We are better off as a team, especially where our strengths and weaknesses balance each other. A good team brings out the best in one another like Gloria and Officer Buckle. "'Friendship' is a rather ordinary word, but it carries extraordinary significance in our lives," Sol Gordon says in his book, *Is There Anything I Can Do?* The real test came one day after Officer Buckle saw his speech on television and realized it was Gloria's antics that kept people engaged. He felt awful. When the next request came in, Officer Buckle turned it down. When the school asked if Gloria could come instead, she went by herself. At Gloria's solo

Safety Speech, the strangest thing happened! Gloria just sat there, and the children fell asleep again. Afterwards, Officer Buckle received more letters from students. One letter in particular reminded him of the truth, "Gloria missed you yesterday." This realization led to his best safety tip of all, "Safety tip #101: Always stick with your buddy."

"Like most things worthwhile in life, real friendship isn't given to us unchallenged and free of obstacles," Sol Gordon reminds us. Gloria and Officer Buckle were going to have to work through the discomfort Officer Buckle felt. He needed to be reminded that they had a successful history as a team and that it was worth preserving. "The longer we keep our friends, the more history we accumulate and share together. The more friends see and accept our vulnerable side, our imperfections, the richer and dearer the friendships become," Sol Gordon wisely says. This was true of Officer Buckle and Gloria, but even more true for you and I as we evaluate our genuine friendships.

We teach our children to stick together: buddy tags at the beach, buddy benches at school, take a friend with you to the bathroom at public places, don't walk home alone. Even the animals on the ark went two by two! So as adults, we also need our buddies. Where could you use a buddy? When attending something new—a class, a parent meeting, a neighborhood event? What about a presentation at work? Would it be better with a buddy? A double date? A gym workout? Several years ago, one of my dear friends went through a terrible divorce. When the final court appearance arrived, she didn't want to go alone. My friend asked me to be her buddy that day when she went to court. It was sad and scary and official. Having me there gave her courage to do it.

So what if you don't have a buddy? How do you get one? It's probably easiest to assume everyone wants a buddy. (No one has yet asked me to be their running buddy, but let's be honest—I think my 5K days are over.) And someone has to make the first step. Remember, we are better together. Gloria and Officer Buckle weren't effective until they were paired up. Each had gifts the other needed. What about your gifts? Who might be a good match for you?

"The [friends] who support the aspects of our identities that matter the most are the ones we are most likely to count among our collection of good friends," says Dr. Suzanne Degges-White in her article, "Friendology: The Science of Friendship." It's important for us also to examine our relationships from time to time, weighing how friends support our truest selves. The one factor that is a "must-have" in relationships, according to Dr. Suzanne Degges-White, is mutual respect. These are such important reminders for us as grown-ups too.

Evaluate your buddies because not all friendships need to be at the level of Officer Buckle and Gloria, but those that you want to have that teammate quality—such as a running buddy—definitely should!

*Other books like this one:

Swimmy by Leo Lionni

A Sick Day for Amos McGee by Philip C. Stead

CHAPTER 13

Shared Humanity

Blueberries for Sal
by Robert McCloskey

"A good book, he had concluded, leaves you
wanting to reread the book. A great book
compels you to reread your own soul."

–Richard Flanagan, *The Narrow Road to the Deep North*

This timeless story follows a little girl and a little bear helping their mothers collect blueberries for winter. Each little one falls behind her mother as she pauses to eat the berries. While the plot line is simplistic, the implications are more complex. The lessons we learn from these pairs of pickers are of fundamental importance. Although one mother-child pair is two humans and the other is two bears, the similarities and differences between groups of people are readily overlaid.

The essence of being alive and having the same basic needs and desires sit at the root of this story…at the root of all of our stories. If we hope to be the change we wish to see in the world, we have to see a similar goal. We have to see and believe that other people are as human as we are. It sounds easier than history has shown.

This endearing and beautifully illustrated classic tells a parallel story of a mother and young child opposite a mother bear and young cub. Both pairs are picking blueberries on the same mountain. Both have similar methods. The structure of the story is filled with lines and phrases that are nearly exactly like what the other mother says and does. As both youngsters fall behind, they end up switching places. Little Sal follows mother bear while Little Bear follows Little Sal's mother. All of this is unbeknownst to their mothers who continue collecting berries ahead of them. "Little Bear and Little Sal's mother and Little Sal and Little Bear's mother were all mixed up with each other among the blueberries on Blueberry Hill."

Line after line is nearly identical: action for action, both the mothers and their young ones behave with such verisimilitude that they become nearly interchangeable, which is exactly the lesson for us. When we realize how similar we are, how our feelings can be linked, and that our commonalities are greater than our differences, we are at a crucial moment of empathy and relationship. Empathy is the most critical thing for all of us in working towards unity in humanity. As artist and humanitarian Ai Weiwei says, "You begin to understand that we all have the same basic needs, that our sense of humanity and integrity, our desire for warmth and safety, to be well-treated and respected are the same." If we can all learn to see the heart of a person instead of merely their appearances, what a difference we'd make in our divided world!

In Robert McClosky's 1948 treasure, the moment of surprise and delight takes place when the mother bear turns around and sees the child, Little Sal, following her instead of her own cub. Mother Bear's face says quite a bit! She's shocked but calmly backs away from the situation and reroutes her path to find her own cub. Instead of responding with fear, acting out in anger, or scolding, she focuses on what matters more—the safety of her little one.

When we encounter someone who feels like the

"other," what is our response? Curiosity and connection? Or caution and concern? In this story, both mothers, with admirable calm, focus their energy on the well-being of their children. Both mothers respond by de-escalating the situation and perhaps, in some mother-to-mother connection, employ empathy rather than attack. Robert McClosky expertly describes the human mother as "shy of bears" rather than scared of them or desiring to hurt them. She isn't angry at them for being in her territory, doesn't see them as enemies of her people, or assume their intentions are to prey on her young. The author helps us to transcend appearance and connect with the other mother heart-to-heart.

Maya Angelou's poem, *Human Family*, explains this very idea, "We are more alike, my friends, than we are unalike." Her lyrical and image-filled poem describes the similarities and differences of people across all places, but reminds us that, "In minor ways we differ, in major we're the same."

What a message! What a truth! In this story, we see it so clearly on the page. While the characters are bears and people, the lesson may be stark at first, but the parallel structure of Robert McCloskey's events and dialogue shows that in fact, "we are more alike, than we are unalike." So I challenge you to take a look at your perceptions of others because "how we look at other people very often tells us about ourselves," says Ai Weiwei. What do you see when you look at people who are different than you? Consider the truth about who it reveals you to be.

*Other books like this one:
The Day You Begin by Jacqueline Woodson
We Are Not Friends by Anna Kang

CHAPTER 14

Injustice

Ron's Big Mission
by Rose Blue and Corinne J. Naden

———————

"A good book is never finished—
it goes on whispering to you from the wall."
–Virginia Wolff

"Do you know what today is?" I asked my 5-year-old daughter. "Today is the day we're going to get your library card!"

"Yay! I am so excited!" she squealed from the backseat.

This was such a special moment for the two of us. For Liesel, it was thrilling because she could read, write her name, and have something of her own to connect her with the library, a place we both loved. The library erupted in cheers as she received her very first library card. She got a special button and stickers and we took lots of pictures. Liesel has always been a voracious reader. She (quite literally) devoured her board books as a toddler! Our love of reading joins us with a community of readers across time and space. For this reason, *Ron's Big Mission* was an instant favorite in my house.

Ron is the library's best customer, reading there day in and day out. "Mrs. Scott, [the librarian] thought about all the times that Ron came into the library and all the times he sat at the tables for hours looking over so many books." Ron's appetite for reading is exciting and resonates with those of us who read as we breathe. One of my own personal mottos is "so many books, so little time." Yet it is this very desire that leads to obstacles for Ron.

When the story takes place, "only white people [could] check out books from the library." And on this particular day, Ron has had enough. He sets out from his house to check out his library books for himself. As a reader, as a mother, as a human, I am cheering for Ron! With all the confidence that what he is doing is right, Ron approaches the counter and tells the clerk he wants to check out the books. She reminds him of the rules, but Ron is undeterred. He takes it a step farther and jumps on the counter as he restates his request to check out the books.

As I wish so many of us would do when we truly believe in a cause, he refused to back down. When the policemen arrive, even *they* offer to check the book out for him, thinking all he wants is the book. They remind him of the rules. "But Ron just shook his head—he would not budge." The injustice of the situation is heightened even more when his mother is called in to talk Ron down. She says, "I know how you feel, baby…but you have to follow the rules." And then Ron says it for everyone who has ever been oppressed, "I can't, Momma…It's wrong. The rules are not fair. Why can't I check out books like everyone else?" This tenacity, this confidence, this pushing back against injustice is incredible! And then, the librarian writes him a library card and checks out his books. Because of Ron's courage, Mrs. Scott, the librarian, developed courage to do what was right.

Where can we stand up to injustice? Where can our courage inspire others to do what is right? Where can we do the right thing? Perhaps you are just now thinking about places where you enjoy privileges where others might not.

An incredible collection of children's poems, *Can I Touch Your Hair,* by Irene Latham and Charles Waters has two poems in the middle, "Forgiveness" and "Apology." These two poems express some of our fears and missteps in an effort to grow. They are another great place to start addressing injustices in your life. What can you do to heighten your own awareness? Can this book of poems and Ron's courage create empathy for generations of oppressed people? What would that look like? If the courage of one boy with his love of the library can inspire a town, and a book, and me, what might Ron inspire you to do today?

The library card was just the beginning of challenging injustice and pursuing his dreams. The book is based on a true story, and Ron's story continued in real life. Ron became an astronaut as part of the first class of black American astronauts in 1978. And in 1986, Ron was onboard the space shuttle Challenger—he lost his life in that devastating explosion. But because of Ron's courage to "walk over the edge" as he said, he realized his dreams.

This chapter is for all who are afraid to challenge the status quo, afraid to fight for something that matters to you. It's for those who have resigned to let the rules tell you how far you can go. But maybe after reading about Ron, you might be inspired to stand up on the desk and question the injustices in your life. Because, as author Austin Channing Brown says, "All it has ever taken was the transformed—the people of color confronting past and present to imagine a new future, and the handful of white people willing to release indifference and join the struggle." Will you?

*__Other books like this one:__

The Other Side by Jacqueline Woodson
What Do You Do with a Voice Like That? by Chris Barton

CHAPTER 15

The Virtue of Delayed Gratification

A Chair for My Mother
by Vera B. Williams

———

"There is more treasure in books than in
all the pirate's loot on Treasure Island."
–Walt Disney

This book is my mom's favorite. There's something endearing about the three generations of women living together in their little apartment. The hardworking Mama works as a waitress at a little diner every day until her feet get sore. What I always loved about this story was the idea of saving and waiting for something. I loved watching the jar of quarters and nickels grow fuller and fuller. I loved the way everyone chipped in, making it feel like the chair belonged to all who helped Rosa and her mother.

Rosa's family needed a new chair because they had recently lost everything in a fire. As Rosa tells it, they are going to get "a wonderful, beautiful, fat, soft armchair. We will get one covered in velvet with roses all over it. We are going to get the best chair in the whole world." Rosa wants this chair so badly for her mother because her mother works so hard on her feet every day.

While their neighbors did pitch in to donate furniture after their fire, they didn't have anything new or nearly comfortable enough for them. So rather than beg for money or lose hope, the three strong women—Rosa, her mother, and her grandmother—made a plan. "When we can't get a single other coin into the jar, we are going to take out all the money and go and buy a chair." What a wonderful goal. This will require all the extra money they have to be put away, denying any extra spending, or anything above their usual needs so that in the future they will have this chair. Vera Williams explains, "*A Chair for My Mother* is also an expression of my life experience at the moment I was making it. I had finally come to a point in my life where I needed to make a living. My jar was empty! So the book is about Rosa's story and my story, too."

In writing about Vera Williams' books, editor Leonard Marcus says, "As an author and illustrator for children, she has created picture books of rare emotional depth, crafting stories that, unlike most of those to be found in contemporary picture books, do not take the material well-being of their heroes for granted. Because Williams' recurring character, young Rosa, and her family and friends cannot have everything they want they must decide what matters most to them. As they make their choices we come to know them all the better—and ourselves as well." This conscious viewpoint more realistically reflects the situation of most people today. Most people have to make sacrifices and delay some of their desires in order to make ends meet. How many of us saved up to buy a new bike, a car, attend college, or take a trip?

We currently live in a time when money is so much less tangible, it's electronic, it's on a card, it's on credit. We have not delayed gratification, but instead developed delayed consequences for that instant gratification. This is to our country's detriment! Instead of going without things we would enjoy now—being able to afford it in the future and owning it outright—we use credit to buy it now. Then when the bill is due, we sometimes fail to handle it wisely. One of the lessons from this tender family story is that there is such satisfaction in saving for something and the sweetness in acquiring it in due time. It is a valuable lesson to be able do without right now for the long term. In Walter Mischel's book, *The Marshmallow Test,* he discusses the causes of successful delay of gratification and future life success. "While much of what makes self-control less effortful is pre-wired, much of it remains open to learning. The cognitive and emotional skills that make it possible for preschoolers to wait for a bigger reward pave the way for them to develop the psychological resources, mind-sets, and social relationships that can improve their chances to build the fulfilling and successful lives they want." This is hopeful for us as well.

Many young people unused to delayed gratification fail to understand the lesson in this story. Some ask why Rosa's family doesn't just buy all the things they needed to replace what was lost. In a world where credit cards and digital pay make finances seem like a game and turn financial responsibility into a joke, we need the lessons from *A Chair for My Mother.*

Filling the jar to buy the chair is also special because it's a common goal. Each woman contributes with everyone's best interests at heart, but mostly the benefit is for the one who works the hardest—the Mama. This is exactly how Rosa maintains her saving mentality. Like Walter Mischel says in *The Marshmallow Test*, "If you want to decide how something will feel in the future, you might try to imagine yourself doing it in the present." Rosa details how uncomfortable they all are at the end of the day sitting around the kitchen table on hard chairs. Then she dreams about that fat, soft armchair covered in velvet and roses. By seeing how it will feel and drawing a vivid image of that chair in her mind, she is able to forgo the temptations of the present for the future comfort. We, too, ought to try that.

It's a story not of self*fish*ness: "I want this now for me," but one of self*less*ness: "I want a chair for my mother, and we're all going to work for it." It's not flashy or always fun to delay our gratification, or save for the future. It requires sacrifice. Let this charming book remind you to save for what truly feeds your deeper needs. Consider the lesson of delayed gratification like Rosa. You might find your red velvet rose-covered armchair is closer than you think.

*Other books like this one:
Alexander, Who Used to Be Rich Last Sunday by Judith Viorst
When Times Are Tough by Yanitzia Canetti
Pennies in a Jar by Dori Chaconas

CHAPTER 16

Family

Julius, The Baby of the World
by Kevin Henkes

———————

"To read a book for the first time is to
make a new acquaintance; to read it for
a second time is to meet an old friend."

–Chinese proverb

The relationships bound by blood can often leave us the bloodiest. Family ties are forever and nearly-unbreakable despite our occasional wishes otherwise. In Kevin Henkes' family drama, *Julius, the Baby of the World,* delightfully difficult big sister Lilly instantly dislikes her new little brother. She didn't always feel this way. While her mother was pregnant with her baby brother, she was thrilled. "Before Julius was born, Lilly was the best big sister in the world." She gave him gifts and sang to him before bed. Lilly loved the *idea* of a baby brother.

I know that when growing up, I romanticized notions of big families and extended family living nearby. My family of five was the only part of our family tree located in Wisconsin. My parents had arrived in Milwaukee for medical training with no other family members in sight. We spent holidays with church family and friends and a random assortment of people with no place to celebrate, who my mother always took in. This was not my idea of family. I dreamed of cousins running around, old ladies cooking in the kitchen, shared family jokes, and late nights of games. I loved the thought of a big family so much that in my high school senior speech I claimed that when I grew up I wanted ten children and a farm! Ha! (It only took me three kids to need medication and therapy to realize the folly of that idea!) This rosy notion did not equip me for the realities of being the grown-up in a family. "We need to get past abstract nostalgia for traditional family values and develop a clearer sense of how past families actually worked and what the different consequences of various family behaviors and values have been," Historian and author Stephanie Coontz says in *The Way We Never Were*. This is true for Lilly and for us.

When I look back at my eighteen-year-old self, I think what I longed for was a greater connection with people who knew me and who would always be around. But nothing has sent me to therapy more often than my family of origin, the family I married into, and the family I created! So what's wrong with me? Nothing, it turns out.

We long to be loved unconditionally and eternally. We all want to be where someone loves us best of all. For many of us, we dream that is in a family. And for some of us, it is. But family takes some getting used to, some working around and through, and some acceptance. Like Lilly, we don't fall in love with our family immediately nor do we always stay that way.

"After Julius was born, it was a different story…She pinched his tail. And she yelled insulting comments into his crib. 'I am the queen,' said Lilly. 'And I hate Julius.'" Lilly has found that younger siblings need a lot of time and attention. Lilly used to be the center of attention because she was the only child, but no longer is. It's not what she wanted. If we're honest, for some of us, family is this way. "Seeing our family pains as part of a larger social predicament means that we can let ourselves—or our parents—off the hook. Maybe our personal difficulties are not *all* our family's fault; maybe our family's difficulties are not *all* our personal fault," Stephanie Coontz also says.

The other side of this coin—the romantic part—is captured in the book, *The Relatives Came,* by Cynthia Rylant. The pictures are full of love and life, and the words are of eager anticipation with too few days spent together just playing and laughing. I love that idea. But that isn't always the case for any family. A few of my family get-togethers have ended with hurt feelings, silent treatments, and bitterness.

I think Lilly's story captures some of both. There is great fondness and appreciation for family as a group of connected and engaged people who want to be together. But when Lilly's vision doesn't match up to reality, she gets mad. I can relate. Many of my friends have sisters who live nearby. The close proximity and close relationships include sharing childcare duties, weekly get-togethers, and shared outfits. For me, while I have a sister in the greater Milwaukee area, we are not close and it bothers me. The book continues with all the ways Lilly expresses her anger towards Julius and her parents. She even attempts to imitate Julius and gets scolded for it.

This bad behavior continues until the day of Julius'

baby party, with all of their family gathered together. Lilly loudly declares that Julius is "disgusting" and a "silly lump," but when her Cousin Garland voices her negative opinion about Julius, Lilly abruptly changes her tune. No one can insult her brother and get away with it! She orders Cousin Garland to admire, kiss and stroke Baby Julius, and chant as her parents often do, "Julius is the Baby of the World!" It appears that we can criticize and torment our own family but the minute an outsider tries it, they are doomed. There is a tale in our family told now with relish about an incident where my younger cousin bit me on the arm for some offense. Immediately, my sister grabbed his arm and sunk her teeth into it. No one could hurt me and get away with it!

If there is one lesson I have learned about family it is that it's messy, but it is also a blessing. It's both. Some of my memories of extended family gatherings include everyone—cousins, aunts and uncles, and grandparents—all sitting around the old-fashioned ice cream maker taking turns cranking the handle and telling stories and laughing. The memories may be sepia-toned, but they remind me that family can be fun—kind of like what Lilly felt about family before Julius came. Then there are other memories of storming out of the room, doors slamming, and years of silence between siblings, things Lilly felt *after* Julius came.

"Dealing with family issues is a lifelong process of

learning and discovery. Remember, the goal is not to have a perfect family but rather a sense that with each passing year you are making some progress in how you connect with these complex people who are a crucial part of your journey in life," author Leonard Felder offers this advice in his book, *When Difficult Relatives Happen to Good People.* Sometimes it feels easier to avoid family or to make excuses not to attend a gathering. You can only avoid family for so long though. Consider taking action and seeing yourself as part of the family rather than just seeing them as difficult, awkward, annoying, weird, or obnoxious people with the same last name.

Another piece of advice from my own psychologist that I find actually works is to remember that, "even if you can't change your relatives, you can significantly change and improve how you respond to them." Like Lilly did when she made Cousin Garland exclaim, "JULIUS IS THE BABY OF THE WORLD!" we might just realize how wonderful they really are.

*Other books like this one:
Louise Loves Art by Kelly Light
Gaston by Kelly DiPucchio
The Relatives Came by Cynthia Rylant

CHAPTER 17

Dealing With Surprises

This Book Just Ate My Dog
by Richard Byrne

———————

"Good books don't give up all their secrets at once."
–Stephen King

When something crops up in the middle of your life or, in this case, the middle of your book, you face certain options. The curiously titled and absurd story *This Book Just Ate My Dog* follows a young girl, Bella, whose dog suddenly disappears. In a roundabout and silly way, her story teaches us what we can do when the unexpected happens. "Bella was taking her dog for a stroll across the page when something very odd happened." The illustrations make this even funnier. Half of Bella's dog has disappeared from view. It looks as though he's fallen into the crease in the center of the book. While this shocks Bella, it doesn't instantly create the sense of panic that you or I would expend in a similar situation.

On the next page, our heroine is left holding only the dog's leash! The way Bella processes her situation and successfully employs a plan to get her dog back are worthwhile lessons. While we might not have our dogs disappear into the fold of a paperback book, we will very likely live a life filled with unexpected surprises. Some will be positive and others quite negative. Our responses to these incidents speak to our adaptability, and our adaptability largely determines how we fare once the dust settles.

M.J. Ryan offers advice on how to deal with unexpected circumstances in her sweetly instructive book, *AdaptAbility*. "Since we live in a changing universe, why do [humans] oppose change?" Change is the one thing you can count on.

In Richard Byrne's quirky story, Bella has to quickly

change her expectations and course of action in order to rescue her dog and continue their walk. If Bella had merely stood there stuck in fear about the change to her plans or evaluating her options without taking action, the dog might have been lost forever. Or Bella might have been waiting on the sidewalk holding a leash for hours.

When facing an unexpected change of plans, M.J. Ryan says step one is to accept the change. "The best first thing we can do rather than stick our heads in the sand is get clear on what is actually happening so we can get down to the business of dealing with it…otherwise we can't respond in the most productive manner." She then suggests that we get the facts and, if further questions remain, get more information and seek answers.

We see this in Bella's response. Despite the ridiculousness of the situation, Bella sees what has happened. The book ate her dog. She knows it has happened and she accepts that this is the situation she now faces. Then, again modeling excellent adaptability, Bella tells a friend, "This book ate my dog." She is straightforward with the facts that are available to her. Her caring friend, Ben, decides to investigate. One of the worst feelings in the world is believe you are alone in your mess. If you think it's up to you to fix it or survive it, you can easily despair.

During a season of personal darkness and depression, I needed help from all sorts of friends. I needed friends to pick me up off the bathroom floor when I laid there wanting desperately to die. In my suicidal state, I needed good friends to watch me and my kids—I couldn't be left alone. Our dear friends brought meals since I wasn't cooking or even eating. We had friends who encouraged my husband as he tried to take care of us all, wrestling with feelings of helplessness and fear that one day he'd find me unresponsive or worse, dead. If not for those kind and generous people, I likely wouldn't be here today. If you have ever been in a struggle and been offered help you know it takes tremendous humility to accept it, and yet many of us keep help at arm's length.

Bella shows us a different way. She lets her friend help, she lets the professionals help, and then she uses her own talents to remedy the predicament. But she's never alone.

M.J. Ryan says that for many of us, we see these surprises and deny that they are upsetting. We want the problem resolved immediately and smoothly. However, that might not be the best way to view these changes. She wisely counsels that change not of your choosing often sets off an emotional process that experts say follows a predictable cycle much like the five stages of grief. So be gentle with yourself, and take Bella's actions as an example.

Bella does not dismiss the situation or its solution as an impossible circumstance. She accepts the mess she's in and persists in finding a way out. In this way, Bella reminds us to stay open for the possibility of miracles, expand our options, tap into our inner talents, take action, and always keep hope alive. Bella's resourceful and humorous solution is to send a letter out from the middle of the book to the reader with instructions for getting the book to give up its prisoners. And with a few steps, they all tumble back onto the page! "We're all survivors of our own lives. You've dealt with changes you never anticipated or wanted and despite your best efforts there are no guarantees you won't have to keep on doing it. Despite it all, you're still here! You've made it so far, and that's pretty good evidence that you will continue to, even if some days you don't know how," M.J. Ryan encourages us. That's a relief!

Bella's strategies are practical and relatable. We may think that our lives are over when we meet surprise circumstances that derail our plans, but M.J. Ryan reminds us that some people avoid change at all costs questioning our capacity to survive it. "Research shows that not only do we have the ability to grow through the challenges of our life, what experts call post-traumatic growth, but the benefits of doing so include improved relationships, new possibilities for our lives, a greater appreciation for life, a greater sense of personal strength and spiritual development." Have you ever experienced this? If you have lived even twenty years on this Earth then you have probably met situations and circumstances that you didn't ask for. How did you handle them? In hindsight, would you handle them differently?

Before I began writing this book, I had a brief stint in a part-time role at our church. It seemed to be everything I wanted in a new job, and I jumped in with tremendous enthusiasm. Within three months, I resigned. The job description was vague and my new ideas were misunderstood. It was an ill-suited position for me, but I didn't see that coming when I started it. "Now what?" I wondered. In this unforeseen space, I waited. And after a few months, this book began to emerge. If we are adaptable, something good will come.

M.J. Ryan's book and Bella's story both teach us to see a hard situation with positive perspective. M.J. Ryan recommends humor. "People who thrive during change work in their funny bones." At our house, we say there are always two responses: you can cry about it or you can laugh about it. We continually choose to laugh. My hope is that when you find yourself in the midst of unexpected change, with circumstances you did not ask for, you will remember Bella's path. Perhaps your surprise will lead to a pleasant place, a better-than-before result, or even a charming book.

*Other books like this one:

I Want My Hat Back by Jon Klassen
One Cool Friend by Toni Buzzeo
This Moose Belongs to Me by Oliver Jeffers

CHAPTER 18

Knowing When Enough Is Enough

King Bidgood's in the Bathtub
by Audrey Wood

———————

"I think books are like people, in the sense that they'll
turn up in your life when you most need them."

–Emma Thompson

Sometimes you gotta call the game. But how do you know when it's time to quit? How do you know when you've had enough? Audrey and Don Wood's delightful and beautifully illustrated tale of a King who won't leave his tub in order to rule his kingdom is a silly example of someone who doesn't know when enough is enough. (I'm sure that if I stayed in the tub more than an hour, and didn't rule my household, my skin would begin to slough off and my kids would be fighting and destroying things.)

The story begins with the young page crying to the castle-folk, "Help, help! King Bidgood's in the bathtub and he won't get out! Oh, who knows what to do?" While this story revels in the absurdity of such a situation, the tendency to hang on longer than we ought to convinces me that King Bidgood may be more like us than we know.

Are you the friend who doesn't know when to stop talking? Or when to dump the boyfriend? Or when to stop complaining? Or when to quit that miserable job? Daniel Pink's book, *When*, suggests that timing is everything, proposing that there are ideal times—both of day and in life—to tackle certain tasks. Daniel Pink says that endings can be particularly tricky for us because we tend to imbue them with great significance. Instead of avoiding the end we ought to, "integrate our perspectives on time into a coherent whole, one that helps us comprehend who we are and why we're here." In *King Bidgood's in the Bathtub*, the unfortunate and central character of this story delays the end of his bath until someone else brings the day to a close for him by opening the drain. Consider what ending you are putting off.

"What's hard for human beings is letting go. We are, as the Nobel Prize-winning work of Daniel Kahneman famously showed, a conservative and loss-aversive bunch," Peg Streep says in her article for *Psychcentral.com*. While we all manifest our feelings about endings on a spectrum of willingness, it is important to keep in mind our general sticking points when it comes to knowing when to quit. Peg Streep discusses one common bias that keeps people stuck: the sunk cost fallacy in which we tend to think only of the time we've already put into something rather than what more we will lose if we continue on this path. This fallacy "has you focused on time already spent—which is by definition irretrievable—and keeps you from imaging where you might be in the future." For our character, King Bidgood, he is focused on his comfort of the moment and the current condition instead of the potential for greater enjoyment outside of the tub and in the future. We may need to step back and evaluate where we might be staying-put too long whether from fear or fallacy.

While projecting yourself into future opportunities is essential for successful quitting, be advised that the transition will bring stress. "If what you are thinking of quitting is central to your self-definition, you need to be prepared. For example, if your career and the rewards you've reaped from it are central to your self, change will be harder than it would be for someone who is not mainly invested in that arena and defines himself or herself by numerous roles in addition," says Peg Streep.

This is exactly what happened to me when I quit teaching to stay home with our daughter. Although I had not planned on quitting, circumstances led to that within a matter of weeks while I was on maternity leave. If someone had given me this advice prior to that transition, I might not have lapsed into severe anxiety and eventual depression. I was an English teacher, and I was good at it. My students were impacted by my work, and that work defined me. While I knew that staying home with Liesel was the right decision for our family at the time, it could have gone more smoothly in terms of how I processed my resignation.

Where do you find yourself needing to pull back? Are you thinking of quitting a job, releasing a commitment, or walking away from a relationship? Are you afraid? Are you aware of your options? What appeals have people tried to get you to quit?

In this story, the Knight is the first to try to get the King out, plying him with talk of battle! In spite of the gravity of the call for the leadership of the King, he remains unconvinced. He is more persuasive than the Knight and is already set up for playing at battle in the bath. Reluctantly, they play and the King refuses to get out. Only the Knight emerges, dripping wet and beaten. For the Knight, the cost of confronting the King was humiliation. In the King's refusal to know when enough is enough, he mistreated his employee. How do you treat others when they tell you hard truths? Do you listen or do you remain in your own world, convinced of your own rightness? Consider this story before you ignore those who aim to help you.

The next confrontation comes from his wife, the Queen. She marches in to coerce him out of the tub by appealing to his stomach, "It's time to lunch!" Again, the King is unconvinced and, instead, gives her the run around by having lunch served in the tub. The King is sidetracked and overly optimistic about the quality and quantity of food and its ability to pacify his wife's demand that he get out of the tub. Some of us are, unfortunately, easily lured to remain in place by simple pleasures rather than considering the appropriateness of listening and respecting our spouse's or others' requests.

The third attempt to get the King to quit the bath is the Duke, who appeals to him using his hobby of fishing without success. The night comes on and the King still remains in the tub. The final attempt is from the whole crew. The court all come in pleading and appealing to his sense of fun—a masquerade ball! Yet in all these attempts, the King fails to heed warnings, fails to see things from his friends' perspective and doesn't know when enough is enough. His sense of timing is completely skewed.

Once you have decided to make changes, unlike King Bidgood, be careful that you don't leave in an overly reactive moment. Don't burn bridges. "Remember that quitting isn't an end in and of itself; it's a pathway to a new destination," says Peg Streep. In this quite silly story, there are many perspectives to consider, and we must examine our potential roles.

Are you constantly thinking of your needs and desires? Could someone be trying to tell you some hard truth, or do you just have trouble with endings? If it's hard for you to let go and make a leap to anywhere or anything else, then this book is for you. If you don't listen to others' calls, then perhaps it's time to heed the advice of this story lest you be caught bare, embarrassed, and alone like King Bidgood.

Perhaps you are not the King remaining deaf to the pleas of those around you, but are you perhaps the friend trying to confront someone? If you are the messenger tasked with delivering a hard truth, here are some methods to try: appeal to their duty, their stomach, their sense of fun. Unfortunately, all of these appeals may still fall dead on arrival.

If that is true, maybe it's time to try a little trick like the page boy in the story and simply pull the plug.

*Other books like this one:
Cloudy With a Chance of Meatballs by Judi Barrett
Stuck by Oliver Jeffers
Pinkalicious by Victoria Kann

CHAPTER 19

Generosity

Extra Yarn
by Mac Barnett

———————

"I think it's the books that you read when
you're young that live with you forever."
–J.K. Rowling

The generosity of children should shame us as adults. As grown-ups, we are too quick to claim something as ours, something we deserve or earned or bought with our own money, something we believe we are entitled to call our own. But like these most-excellent stories do, the children's story of *Extra Yarn* teaches even adults the power of generosity. Mac Barnett tells the story of a cold, bleak town where a little girl named Annabelle finds a box filled with colorful yarn. She knits herself a sweater but finds that "she had some extra yarn," so she begins to knit sweaters for others.

Annabelle's joy in generosity earns the attention of others. So she begins to knit for the jealous neighbor boy, Nate, for her distracted classmates and frustrated teacher and all of the townspeople. And there was always extra yarn. She made sweaters for all the animals, too. "Soon, people thought, soon Annabelle will run out of yarn. But it turned out she didn't." Encouraged by the difference these sweaters made in the lives of the townspeople, she continues to bring joy in sharing her excess. Annabelle made sweaters for things in the town that didn't even wear sweaters—things like houses, mailboxes, and trees, coloring her dreary little village. The more Annabelle knit, the more "things began to change in that little town."

Annabelle's generosity brought joy to her and her community. Acts of generosity can make the darkness of our world feel more hopeful. Even though Annabelle only had a box of yarn to share, she shared it anyway. You don't have to be the richest person or the smartest person to share what you have. Annabelle had no idea how much she really had to give, but that didn't hold her back. "You may have much to give, or you may have only a little to give. The key to the power of giving is giving to your potential. The first step toward reaching your potential is determining what you have that could be of value to others. You may have more than you think," Azim Jamal and Harvey McKinnon say in their book, *The Power of Giving.*

Word got around, and people from near and far came to meet the little girl with the yarn. Annabelle's example of generosity changes everyone and everything—her generosity is contagious. This is the ripple effect of an act of kindness. Most of the time we will have no idea if our sharing has made any difference. Generosity impacts the recipient and also changes the giver.

Later on in the book, Annabelle is robbed of her box of yarn. Yet in spite of this horrible theft, the gift of generosity and the changes it brought to the town, and to Annabelle herself, could not be taken away. The archduke who stole the box was angered when he found it empty, cursing Annabelle with unhappiness. But that's the best thing about being generous: no one can steal your happiness from you. It's a condition of the heart. And when the box of yarn winds its way down the river right back to Annabelle, we see that the giver always gains.

In *The Generosity Bet,* author William High says that we all have an "innate desire to be part of something lasting, something important, something significant…and a life marked by generosity is a life that will truly make a difference, a life that is significant." Consider this statement for a moment. Annabelle's generosity certainly made a difference. Most of us are yearning to be well-known and do something that matters. What if it's less about us and more about the impact of our generosity towards others? What if we are more like Annabelle and her yarn?

William High shares the story of Pastor Craig Groeschel, founder of one of the largest churches in America. In talking about his own journey of generosity, Pastor Craig Groeschel says that after they decided to give away all their online church content, "giving became contagious." It began to penetrate every corner of their church. As they developed resources, it became standard to give them away. Generosity became a value. As a result of this churchwide act of giving, Pastor Groeschel now says his motto is "Generosity is not something we do—it is something we are." Wow. Could that be said of you and I? Like Annabelle did?

What gift might you be able to share with others? Consider all that you've been given and see where there might be a little extra to give to others. In our family, we know specific children who are the recipients of our hand-me-downs. We enjoy *literally* clothing our neighbors. This month, I received tremendous joy in being able to purchase new uniform clothing for a fourth grader at the school where I volunteer. The child has no idea who was so generous, but the joy of giving continues to impact me.

Maybe for you it's not money. Maybe it's time or talents. Maybe it's like my friend, Kelly, who organized a family serving night at a local homeless shelter. Maybe it's the gift of a smile, tender touch, or a compassionate hug. Or maybe it's clothing your neighbors the way Annabelle did with her extra yarn. Maybe you will see the effects of your giving to others directly. Maybe you will see changes in yourself. Most likely you will see both. The joy of generosity can warm a whole community, just start with your extra yarn.

*Other books like this one:
Should I Share My Ice Cream? by Mo Willems
One Hen by Katie Smith Milway
Boxes for Katje by Candace Fleming

CHAPTER 20

Understanding Your History

Auntie Luce's Talking Paintings
by Francie Latour

_____

"In books I have traveled, not only to
other worlds, but into my own."
–Anna Quindlen

"Our roots claim us in ways we don't even realize," says author and researcher Megan Smolenyak. No matter where you live or where you come from, tracing your family's history is a powerful way to connect with your extended family and, in turn, with your own identity. This vibrantly illustrated and lyrically written story by Francie Latour is set in the hills of tropical Haiti. The colorful landscape paintings are a bold background for the story of this young girl and her journey to discover her unique identity through her family history.

While the young narrator and her family live in a cold, northern region of the U.S., her Auntie Luce lives in warm, tropical Haiti where their family originated. On her yearly visit to her ancestral home, she asks her aunt to paint a portrait of her. This moment is more than a portrait sitting. As she sits, she studies the many paintings in her auntie's studio. There are paintings of grandparents, of history's heroes, and of women of influence. Through each painting, she learns about the people who fought, died, stood up to injustice, and established their freedom. These are the stories that she listens to while sitting for the portrait. The narrator learns about not only her own family's emigration but about the birth of the nation of Haiti.

The young narrator learns, too, about how her Auntie Luce couldn't leave Haiti, how her history lessons in the U.S. regarding wars and slavery and Haiti were incomplete and how, despite living in the U.S., she will always be a part of Haiti, and the land a part of her. These lessons are not unique to this young narrator. In *Who Do You Think You Are,* Megan Smolenyak writes about actress Susan Sarandon's search made for her own family history. Her research pointed to Tuscany, Italy, as the place where Susan Sarandon's ancestor began his immigration journey to the U.S. Susan Sarandon then flew to Florence, Italy to pick up the trail. Strolling through the city, she remarked, "From the first time I came to Italy, I felt inexplicably at home. Now I know why. My gene pool is crying out!" Our familial homeland can offer us tremendous insight into our own identity.

Like the little girl visiting Haiti in *Auntie Luce's Talking Paintings* actress Brooke Shields was also affected deeply by the more complete understanding of her family history through Megan Smolenyak's research. "There is something empowering' about 'being able to find your place in the grand scheme of things,'" Brooke Shields says in *Who Do You Think You Are.* "I now feel much more complete as a person. It's been very freeing to me to realize that I don't have to solely come from one side." She now describes herself as "an amalgamation of all these people and all of these genes and all of these experiences." This is what the young girl in the story realizes, too. Throughout *Auntie Luce's Talking Paintings*, the sights and sounds and smells of

Auntie Luce's hometown in Haiti fill her senses and call to her heart as all of our origin stories can do.

Knowing where we come from helps us realize who we are and provides insight as we decide where to go in life. Do you know where your ancestors originated from? Have you ever wondered about why you do some of the things you do? Why you love cinnamon or hate the cold? Are there parts of your family history that seem mysterious? What if you discovered the reasons why you are the way you are?

"When I started my parents' story, I thought that the story of the family down the street was a better story. I didn't think much of my parents' story," Victor Villasenor tells us in Jim Willard and Harry and Jane Wilson's book, *Ancestors*. When he finally went to his ancestral homeland in Mexico, he said, "I am somebody, I come from somewhere… Now my parents are my greatest heroes…until you get to the roots of your family, you are absolutely lost. Just like a ship out at sea in storms, and you are helpless." Victor Villasenor found peace and gained a fuller understanding of his identity through his family history.

The truth is that in researching your family history "you will find heroes and villains, saints and sinners. You will find yourself." It's vital to remember that not all of our ancestors were great people, however, "it's a matter of focusing on the good ones…being inspired by these relatives…following the footsteps of the ones who left the world a better place," encourages *Ancestors* authors Jim and Terry Willard and Jane Wilson. While the narrator in *Auntie Luce's Talking Paintings* is surrounded by the best examples of her past, we must wrestle also with those who we are less proud of.

In her article, "Your ancestor owned slaves? Don't run from it; tell the kids," CNN correspondent, Kelly Wallace, interviews genealogist and author A.J. Jacobs who says, "What children learn when they hear about their past—both the good and the bad—is primarily that they can chart their own course and don't have to follow the path of what their less-than-stellar ancestors did. They also learn that they are part of something bigger than themselves." These family stories give children a sense of personal identity over time and also help them better understand their place in a larger world. The bonus might be that as A.J. Jacobs noted, the children's discovery of their relatives, "made reading and learning about the family history so much more personal." Like the little girl in *Auntie Luce's Talking Paintings,* we are part of a much larger history. And part of what we learn about ourselves, our identity, is formed by these people and places we may or may not know well.

What family stories do you know? What locations are important to your people? Your story? Do you see personal characteristics that you've inherited from generations before? I recently learned that our family is not as Scottish or Irish as we thought. My aunt used an Ancestry DNA kit and discovered that my dad's side of the family is mainly of German descent! We all got a good chuckle out of that because most of our family have kilts in our clan tartan, and my siblings and I had bagpipes at our weddings. Ironically, I married a man with majority German descent so we named our children Liesel, Hans, and Fritz—good German names. Living in Milwaukee, Wisconsin adds an extra layer since it was founded by five German brewing families and retains a very German culture. One of my children's favorite thing to eat is Bratwurst!

As you go out into this wide world, knowing where you come from helps you stay rooted and strong. So who are you? Maybe now's the time to find out.

*Other books like this one:
Tar Beach by Faith Ringgold
A Different Pond by Bao Phi
The Keeping Quilt by Patricia Polacco

CONCLUSION

If you have enjoyed your return trip to childhood via these timeless books, then I have succeeded. If you see these stories with new eyes and have new inspiration as you move forward in your life, then I have achieved more than I dreamed possible. These twenty books are only a fraction of the incredible trove of picture books out there and the myriad lessons available to us as grown-ups. May you regain your childhood whimsy and add it to your life experiences to make your future rich with new meaning. May you say, as my daughter did, "this one gets me every time."

ACKNOWLEDGMENTS

Thank you to God my Father for my very life and breath and to Jesus Christ my Savior. All of this life is grace.

Thank you, dear husband, Mike. Without your support and encouragement this book wouldn't have happened. My dream didn't die, it just got beat-up and lost. Thank you for helping me find it. Thank you for believing in me when I couldn't even believe in myself.

This book is here because of my children, Liesel, Hans and Fritz. Thank you for loving these books again and again with me. This book is also *for* you, to show you that mothers can do anything!

Thank you to my mother who told me as a child, "you will write a book someday, you are such a reader!" Thank you for being a believer long before I was. Thank you for fueling me constantly with "more input" in any form.

Thank you to Lisa Hurley, my patient and kind first editor.

Thank you also to Kerri Lukasavitz for being an excellent and compassionate writing coach.

Thank you, Orange Hat Publishing. Thank you, Shannon and Kaeley and Kaye and Lauren for making this dream come true.

Thank you, Jon Etter, for advice on writing queries and agents and for proving parenthood and writing aren't mutually exclusive.

To Carly at Café Blue for keeping me caffeinated and giving me a wonderful place to write and for your egg bagel magic.

Thank you to Dr. Jeffrey Davis at Wheaton College who called greatness out of me and taught me how to put myself on the page.

Thank you to my former students for indulging me and for being childlike in your listening to these books.

Thank you to Scholastic Book Orders for making purchasing great books a cheap addiction.

Thank you to The Little Read Book, my local independent bookseller, for keeping the aura of magic in a bookstore.

Thank you to the Wauwatosa Public Library for a clean, well-lit place to do research. And thank you to the children's librarians for stocking such delightful stories.

Thank you to Anne Lamott for shitty first drafts and more.

Thank you to Women Speakers Collective and The Giving Keys, for teaching me to be Fearless.

And lastly, thank you, my readers. May the simple messages of these childhood stories be your handbook for walking in adulthood too.

BIBLIOGRAPHY

Chapter 1:

Aristotle. *Poetics.*

Powell, Esta. "Catharsis in Psychology and Beyond: A Historic Overview."

Viorst, Judith. *Alexander and the Terrible, Horrible, No Good, Very Bad Day.* Simon and Schuster. 1972.

Chapter 2:

Duhigg, Charles. "The Real Roots of American Rage." *The Atlantic:* Jan/Feb, 2019.

Sendak, Maurice. *Where the Wild Things Are.* Harper & Row: 1963.

Chapter 3:

Johnson, Crockett. *Harold and the Purple Crayon.* Harper: 1955.

Kim, K.H. *The Creativity Challenge.: How We Can Recapture American Innovation.* Prometheus Books: New York, New York: 2016.

Chapter 4:

Freeman, Don. *Corduroy.* Viking: 1968.

Pogosyan, Marianna, Ph.D. "How Does Culture Affect Our Happiness?" *Psychology Today.* May, 24, 2016. www.psychologytoday.com.

Chapter 5:

Clayson, Jane. https://www.wbur.org/onpoint/2017/12/28/power-of-perseverance-duckworth. Accessed April 17, 2019.

Duckworth, Angela. *Grit.* Scribner. New York, New York: 2016.

Elleman, Barbara. *Virginia Lee Burton: A Life in Art.* Houghton Mifflin Company: Boston: 2002.

Chapter 6:

Brown, Margaret Wise. *Goodnight Moon.* Harper Collins. New York, New York: 1947.

Stevenson, Shawn. *Sleep Smarter.* Rodale. New York, New York. 2016.

The Sleep Foundation. www.thesleepfoundation.org

Chapter 7:

Brown, Brené. *Dare to Lead.* Penguin Random House. 2018.

Waber, Bernard. *Ira Sleeps Over.* Sandpiper. 1975.

Chapter 8:

Hoban, Russell. *Bread and Jam for Frances.* Harper Collins. 1964.

Sukel, Kayt. *The Art of Risk.* National Geographic. Washington, D.C.: 2016.

Chapter 9:

Braiker, Harriet B. *The Disease to Please.* McGraw-Hill. New York, New York: 2001.

Hoberman, Mary Ann. *The Seven Silly Eaters.* HMH Books for Young Readers. 2000.

Chapter 10:

Conrad, Pam. *The Tub People.* Harper Collins. 1999.

Krznaric, Roman. *Empathy.* Penguin Random House. New York, New York: 2014.

Chapter 11:

de la Peña, Matt. *Last Stop On Market Street.* Penguin Books. 2015.

Kennelly, Stacey. "A Scientific Reason to Stop and Smell the Roses." https://greatergood.berkeley.edu/article/item/ascientific-reason-to-stop-and-smell-the-roses. July 3, 2012. Accessed: May 29, 2019.

Klein, Gary. *Seeing What Others Don't.* Public Affairs. New York, New York: 2013.

Chapter 12:

Degges-White, Dr. Suzanne. "Friendology: The Science of Friendship." www.psychologytoday.com/blog. May 29, 2018. Accessed: May 28, 2019.

Gordon, Sol. *Is There Anything I Can Do?* Delacorte Press. New York, New York: 1994.

Rathmann, Peggy. *Officer Buckle and Gloria.* G.P. Putnam's Sons. New York, New York: 1995.

Chapter 13:

Angelou, Maya. "Human Family." www.allpoetry.com.

McCloskey, Robert. *Blueberrries for Sal.* The Viking Press. New York, New York: 1948.

Weiwei, Ai. *Humanity.* Princeton University Press. Princeton, New Jersey: 2018

Chapter 14:

Blue, Rose and Corinne J. Naden. *Ron's Big Mission.* Dutton Children's Books. New York, New York: 2009.

Brown, Austin Channing. *I'm Still Here: Black Dignity in a World Made for Whiteness.* Convergent. New York, New York: 2018.

Latham, Irene and Charles Waters. *Can I Touch Your Hair?* Carolrhoda Books. Minneapolis, Minnesota: 2018.

Chapter 15:

Marcus, Leonard, editor. *Show Me a Story.* Candlewick. 2012.

Mischel, Walter. *The Marshmallow Test.* Little, Brown and Company. New York, New York: 2014.

Williams, Vera B. *A Chair for My Mother.* Greenwillow Books. New York, New York: 1982.

Chapter 16:

Coontz, Stephanie. *The Way We Never Were.* Harper Collins. New York, New York: 1992.

Felder, Leonard. *When Difficult Relatives Happen to Good People.* Rodale. 2003.

Henkes, Kevin. *Julius, the Baby of the World.* Greenwillow Books. New York, New York: 1990.

Chapter 17:

Byrne, Richard. *This Book Just Ate My Dog!* Henry Holt and Co. 2014.

Ryan, M.J. *Adaptability.* Broadway Books. New York, New York: 2009.

Chapter 18:

Pink, Daniel H. *When.* Riverhead Books. 2018.

Streep, Peg. "Is it Time to End the Relationship? 6 Telltale Signs It Might Be." https://psychcentral.com/

knotted/2019/08/is-it-time-to-end-the-relationship-6-tell-tale-signs-that-it-might-be/. August 2019.

Wood, Audrey. *King Bidgood's in the Bathtub.* Harcourt. San Diego: 1985.

Chapter 19:

Barnett, Mac. *Extra Yarn.* Harper Collins. New York, New York: 2012.

High, William F. *The Generosity Bet.* Destiny Image Publishers, Inc. Shippensburg, Pennsylvania: 2014.

Jamal, Azim and Harvey McKinnon. *The Power of Giving.* Penguin Group. New York, New York: 2005.

Chapter 20:

Latour, Francie. *Auntie Luce's Talking Paintings.* Groundwood Books. 2018.

Smolenyak, Megan. *Who Do You Think You Are?* Viking Press. New York, New York: 2010.

Wallace, Kelly. "Your Ancestor Owned Slaves? Don't Run from It; Tell The Kids." https://cnn.com/2015/06/03/living/telling-kids-family-history-benefits-feat/index. Accessed: July 8, 2019.

Willard, Jim and Terry and Jane Wilson. *Ancestors.* Houghton Mifflin Company. New York, New York: 1997.

Maureen Kasdorf is a former high school English teacher, Sleep Coach, and speaker. She and her husband, Mike, live in Wauwatosa, Wisconsin, with their three spirited elementary-school-aged children and puppy, Sugar. This is her first book.